DIPLOMACY, ADMINISTRATION, AND POLICY:

THE IDEAS AND CAREERS OF

FREDERICK E. NOLTING, JR.
FREDERICK C MOSHER
PAUL T. DAVID

Edited by
Kenneth W. Thompson

Lanham • New York • London

The Miller Center

University of Virginia

Copyright © 1995 by
University Press of America®, Inc.
4720 Boston Way
Lanham, Maryland 20706

3 Henrietta Street
London WC2E 8LU England

All rights reserved
Printed in the United States of America
British Cataloging in Publication Information Available

Copublished by arrangement with
The Miller Center of Public Affairs,
University of Virginia

The views expressed by the author(s) of this publication do not necessarily represent the opinions of the Miller Center. We hold to Jefferson's dictum that: "Truth is the proper and sufficient antagonist to error, and has nothing to fear from the conflict, unless by human interposition, disarmed of her natural weapons, free argument and debate."

Library of Congress Cataloging-in-Publication Data

Diplomacy, administration, and policy : the ideas and careers of Frederick E. Nolting, Jr., Frederick C. Mosher, Paul T. David / edited
by Kenneth W. Thompson.
p. cm.
1. Political scientists--United States--Biography. 2. White Burkett Miller Center--Biography. 3. Nolting, Frederick. 4. Mosher, Frederick C. 5. David Paul Theodore. 6. Public administration. 7. Political science. 8. International relations. I. Thompson, Kenneth W.
JA92.D57   1995   95-6828
320'.092'273--dc20   CIP

ISBN 0-8191-9882-X (cloth: alk paper)
ISBN 0-8191-9883-8 (pbk: alk paper)

⊖™ The paper used in this publication meets the minimum requirements of American National Standard for Information Sciences—Permanence of Paper for Printed Library Materials, ANSI Z39.48–1964.

To

Lindsay C. Nolting

Edith K. Mosher

Opal D. David

Contents

PREFACE ix
   Kenneth W. Thompson

INTRODUCTION xi
   Kenneth W. Thompson

I. INTERNATIONAL RELATIONS: A STUDY IN COMPLEXITY
AMBASSADOR FREDERICK E. NOLTING, JR.

1. **MEMORIAL COLLOQUIUM TO FREDERICK E. NOLTING, JR.** 3
   Friends of Ambassador Nolting

2. **KENNEDY, NATO, AND SOUTHEAST ASIA** 17
   Ambassador Frederick E. Nolting

3. **A PERSONAL APPRECIATION: THE BEGINNINGS OF A REVISIONIST VIEW ON FREDERICK NOLTING** 37
   Kenneth W. Thompson

CONTENTS

II. ADMINISTRATION AND GOVERNANCE
PROFESSOR FREDERICK C. MOSHER

4. THE LEGACY OF FREDERICK C. MOSHER 43
   Max O. Stephenson, Jr. and Jeremy F. Plant

5. THE CHANGING RESPONSIBILITIES AND
   TACTICS OF THE FEDERAL GOVERNMENT 81
   Frederick C. Mosher

6. A TALE OF TWO AGENCIES (THE GENERAL
   ACCOUNTING OFFICE AND THE OFFICE OF
   MANAGEMENT AND BUDGET): THE AGENCIES
   AND THEIR CHANGING MILIEU 103
   Frederick C. Mosher

7. THE PUBLIC SERVICE IN THE
   TEMPORARY SOCIETY 119
   Frederick C. Mosher

8. A PERSONAL APPRECIATION: FREDERICK C.
   MOSHER: THEORIST AND PRACTITIONER 151
   Kenneth W. Thompson

III. POLICY: PRINCIPLES, PROCESS, AND PRACTICE
PROFESSOR PAUL T. DAVID

9. PAUL THEODORE DAVID: IN MEMORIAM 157
   Laurin Henry

CONTENTS

10. **IS IT POSSIBLE TO MOVE TOWARD MORE RESPONSIBLE POLITICAL PARTIES?** 163
    Paul T. David

11. **GOVERNMENT AS AGENT OF SOCIAL CHANGE: SOME PROBLEMS IN THEORY** 173
    Paul T. David

12. **A REVIEW OF THE WORK AT THE CHICAGO CONFERENCE ON INTERNATIONAL AVIATION** 193
    Paul T. David

13. **A PERSONAL APPRECIATION** 229
    Kenneth W. Thompson

Preface

An institution is as strong as those who seek to carry out its purposes. In a very real sense this idea has held true for the Miller Center of Public Affairs. Its professional staff, its university associates and scholars and leaders within its extended Miller Center family taken together have been the driving force of its programs. The Center has benefited greatly from the intellectual resources of the University of Virginia as a whole. It also has also enjoyed advantages in being part of a community that multiplies the university's resources through residents who had retired but are active and acknowledged members of the wider intellectual community. Proximity to Washington and the Jeffersonian tradition, with its emphasis on the individual, help explain the rich concentration of intellectual resources in Charlottesville.

Three major figures from the worlds of scholarship, diplomacy, and business stand out in this regard. The first is Ambassador Frederick Nolting, who served with distinction in Vietnam during a critical stage in American foreign policy. A second is Professor Frederick Mosher, considered by many as the doyen of American students of public administration. The third is Professor Paul David, whose concern for public policy marked his association with the Miller Center, the University of Virginia's Department of Government and Foreign Affairs, and the Brookings Institution. Fortuitously, the continuing interests of the three in international relations and diplomacy, public administration, governance and public policy, and the presidency coincided with major focal points in the Center's programs. They all made lasting contributions to the work of the Center.

Introduction

The history of the social sciences is to a significant degree a debate over a fundamental question: What shall be the focus of study? At the heart of any of the constituent disciplines is the search for a unifying concept or idea to bring order out of chaos in the study of some aspect of human behavior. The need is for an organizing principle to distinguish what is most important from what is of interest but less important. What are the central concerns that merit study and how can they be related to one another?

By the mid-20th century, if not the years before and after World War I, it became clear that the study of government and politics could not be limited to American government. The understanding of national government presupposed a recognition of international affairs. Splendid isolation may have been an option for the United States in the 19th century, although events such as the Spanish-American War brought this policy into question. In the 20th century, the nation became increasingly caught up in interactions that linked it with others in the international community. Investment and trade, politics and diplomacy, arbitration and cooperation required not only a national viewpoint, but a window on the world as well.

Frederick E. Nolting, Jr. was the first director of the Miller Center. He returned to the University of Virginia after a distinguished career in business, banking, and foreign policy. In the pages that follow, his career is described in some detail. He was a lieutenant commander in World War II. His career as a diplomat included 18 years in the Department of State, leaving with the permanent rank of career minister. He was alternate permanent representative and deputy representative to NATO, also concerned with its office of political affairs. In the 1950s, he was a special

INTRODUCTION

assistant to the secretary of state for mutual security affairs. At the United Nations, he was a member of the United States Delegation to the Sixth General Assembly. In 1961, Nolting became U.S. ambassador to Vietnam, a historic appointment in a crisis that evolved into the longest war in our history and an unprecedented defeat for American forces.

Historians are likely to debate American policy in Vietnam for years to come, particularly the important decision to encourage the generals and colonels to initiate the military coup that overthrew the Diem government. Ambassador Nolting had argued that unless we had found better leadership with more support in the villages, we should continue working with Diem. A more popular view in the United States was that Diem's government was autocratic and repressive. It had slaughtered Buddhist bonzes and lost the support of the people. The anti-Diem group allied themselves with the antiwar movement, and the Kennedy administration and the public determined to see democracy come about in Vietnam reinforced this point of view. Anti-Diem thinking led to the idea of a military coup, which was leaked to the public as the view of the administration.

The recently released Foreign Relations of the United States documents for 1961-63 help us see the movement for a coup in a new light. Apparently, it involved a weekend decision made in the absence of President Kennedy and secretaries Rusk and McNamara. The three leaders who ramrodded the decision to instruct Nolting's successor Henry Cabot Lodge to support the coup were Averell Harriman, Roger Hilsman, and Mike Forrestal, with assistance from George Ball. Some parties to the action, for example, Roswell Gilpatric, who was holding the fort for McNamara, approved the decision on the assurance that his boss and Kennedy had given their approval. Nolting defended his view, based on extensive travel throughout the countryside, that Diem was the only leader who could restore independence and order, which was being challenged by the Communists and a small radical wing of the Buddhists. Diem was also the best prospect for the eventual achievement of a regime with some but not all characteristics of democracy. The disorder and chaos that surrounded the decision to support the coup seems evident with a small group acting under the leadership

INTRODUCTION

of Harriman. When Harriman spoke of *our* policy, he did not mean Kennedy's or U.S. policy, but *his* policy.

This evidence uncovered in the record and discussed by more than one revisionist historian helps us understand Nolting's argument. It suggests he had a sounder policy than was known at the time and makes his approach worthy of study not only for Vietnam but for other countries where the claims of nationalism and independence become controlling factors.

Ambassador Nolting's philosophy is well expressed in a colloquium, the text of which is the first item in the international relations section of this volume. The second item is an analysis and defense of his position on Vietnam set forth at the Miller Center by the ambassador.

Part II presents an inquiry into public administration and governance. Inasmuch as the Miller Center, with the encouragement of the donor, selected the American presidency as its principal area for study, concern with the executive branch and its relationship with the other two branches of government soon became self-evident. In the late 1970s, Professor Frederick C. Mosher chose to bring his full-time teaching career to a close. He had been a distinguished professor at four universities (Syracuse, Bologna, Berkeley, and Virginia), but later he wished to devote himself more fully to research and writing. Mosher brought prestige and stature to the Center, which was still in its infancy as a public affairs program. He also brought a lifetime of study of administration and governance. It was not long before his influence over Miller Center graduate students and younger scholars became apparent. One example was Max O. Stephenson, Jr., who co-authored the first chapter in this section entitled "The Legacy of Frederick C. Mosher," reprinted from *Public Administration Review.* Two others were aspiring Ph.D.'s in international relations, David Clinton and Daniel Lang. They were inducted by Mosher into the mysteries of public administration as they joined him in the writing of *Presidential Transitions and Foreign Affairs* (Louisiana University Press, 1987).

Professor Mosher left his imprint on the work of the Miller Center in other ways. About the time he joined the staff, the Center at the behest of its governing council inaugurated a program

INTRODUCTION

that was more action-oriented than its research programs. It created the first of seven national commissions to examine urgent national problems. The first commission, co-chaired by former Virginia governor Linwood Holton and former NBC White House correspondent Ray Scherer, studied the presidential press conference. The salience of the choice is suggested by the decision two decades later by the Kennedy School at Harvard to do a follow-up study. The timeliness of the Center's work is seen in the fact that Reagan press secretary James Brady introduced President Reagan's first press conference by displaying the Center's report. Further, he announced that the Reagan administration intended to follow the recommendations of the commission.

To return to Professor Mosher, no one on the staff of the Miller Center showed greater interest in the commissions. He provided inputs in the form of ideas based on vast experience for each of the commissions. He attended some of their meetings and came forward with helpful ideas about future meetings. Because he was a towering figure in his field, he had the respect of others who had attained similar heights in their chosen arenas. With guests who conducted Forums at the Center, we had much the same response. They knew and revered Mosher, and therefore they respected the programs of the Center.

In addition to important articles written during his tenure at the Center, Professor Mosher published two other books. The one was a substantially revised second edition of *Democracy and the Public Service*. In it, he confronted unfolding issues of the professional state and the role of education in an era of growing specialization. In *Democracy* and in the article "The Public Service in the Temporary Society" (chapter 7 in this volume), Mosher addresses his subject in the context of the unending stream of continuity and change. His other important work in his days at the Miller Center was *A Tale of Two Agencies (The General Accounting Office and the Office of Management and Budget)* (see chapter 6 in the present volume). It is no exaggeration to say that both studies take on many of the characteristics of classic works. It is perhaps too early to give them that designation for the 21st century. Suffice it to say they are studies of a powerful mind bringing to bear the

INTRODUCTION

accumulated knowledge of a lifetime on two fundamental issues that remained with Mosher to the end.

Part II then begins with an authoritative review of the legacy of Frederick C. Mosher by two of his former students, Professors Max O. Stephenson, Jr., of Virginia Polytechnic Institute and State University and Jeremy F. Plant of the Pennsylvania State University-Harrisonburg. This review is followed by three of Mosher's most important papers, each with relevance not only to the past but also the present and the future. We shall return to some personal remembrances of Fritz Mosher in "A Personal Appreciation" (see chapter 8).

Third, we seek to honor the memory of Professor Paul T. David. By the time the Miller Center was established, Paul was recognized as a leading scholar and public servant. In 1933, he was literally the first employee of the Tennessee Valley Authority. Through that assignment, he met one of the great figures of the era in higher education and public service, Floyd W. Reeves. Years later I had the opportunity to study with Professor Reeves of the University of Chicago. Under other tutelage, I had faithfully memorized the principles of administration, including the famous (some said infamous) mnemonic aid *podscorb*, representing planning, organization, and so forth. Reeves brought us out of this quagmire into the strong light of administrative problems and decision making, an arena with which he was intimately familiar. In much the way he had recruited Paul David as his deputy for the President's Committee on Administrative Management in 1937, he offered me a position in 1949 with the commission planning the creation of the State University of New York. If Paul had lacked zeal for public policy, Reeves would have instilled a sense of commitment to public service. What set Reeves apart from most professors of administration was an ability to confront students with real life problems, insisting they had to make hard choices in decision making. Almost 50 years later I can see and hear him chewing on such problems and challenging every student to live with reality. He was not the president of the American Political Science Association nor the author of many books, but he prepared us better than others for the world in which we spend the rest of our lives.

INTRODUCTION

To return to David, Paul co-authored a study entitled *Personnel Administration in the Federal Service* for the Brownlow Committee. It defined the field and the need for change for years to come. Next, he became associate director for the American Council on Education's Commission on Youth. More than once he intervened in Miller Center Forums to remind us of the commission's work. By 1942 he had returned to government on the economics staff of the Bureau of the Budget, where he became the staff specialist for the Bureau and the White House on civil aviation policy. He served as principal secretariat officer for the 1944 international conference at Chicago to plan a postwar regime in aviation (see chapter 12). It was this subject that was his last—and, I believe, he felt his most important—contribution to the Center. It was something that preoccupied him in the last months of his life. Preparatory to it, he transferred to the Department of State and was appointed by President Truman as deputy head of the U.S. delegation to the International Civil Aviation Organization from 1947 to 1950.

In chapter 9, Laurin Henry reviews Paul's research and scholarship. Having written the memorial to Paul that will appear in the *American Political Science Review,* no one is better qualified than Laurin to offer such a review. Dr. Henry also provides a history of Paul's years in the Department of Government and Foreign Affairs at the University of Virginia. On my arrival at U.Va, I was subjected to a somewhat different interpretation of this chapter in Paul's life, and as I read Laurin's contrasting account, I thought back to my experience at the University of Chicago and Northwestern University: *plus ca change, plus c'est la meme chose.* With all of the methodological and philosophical writings on university life, we still have no history that realistically describes the dynamics of a university department.

Paul David remained active until the end of his life. His friends observed him with admiration. What better example for others of a man approaching 90 who retained his zest for life and in particular the life of the mind.

I.

INTERNATIONAL RELATIONS: A STUDY IN COMPLEXITY

Ambassador Frederick E. Nolting, Jr.

CHAPTER ONE

Memorial Colloquium to Frederick E. Nolting, Jr.[*]

FRIENDS OF AMBASSADOR NOLTING

NARRATOR: Our Memorial volume brings together colloquia, papers, conversations, and writings in memory of Ambassador Frederick E. Nolting, Professor Paul T. David, and Professor Frederick C. Mosher. The first selection is a conversation that we think Ambassador Nolting would have found memorable—a colloquium among old friends. The selection rests on a simple assumption. We celebrate the life and works of Ambassador Nolting best by revisiting four of the areas in which he made important contributions.

The approach is one of substance, and one can imagine Fritz intervening when he felt one or another speaker didn't have it just right. His interventions always came with a smile and the grace we associate with life in Virginia and the university that Paul Freund of the Harvard Law School called "the last remaining citadel of civility."

---

[*]*A Memorial Colloquium held at the Miller Center on 12 November 1991 in honor of Frederick E. Nolting, Jr., director of the Miller Center from 1975 to 1978. Participants included Ambassadors Lucius B. Battle, William E. Colby, and Edwin Martin; Mr. Hal Ford; Mr. Murat Williams; and Mr. Kenneth W. Thompson as narrator.*

The four areas that seem closest to Ambassador Nolting's life and works are American foreign policy, Vietnam and defense, intelligence, and the economy of Europe—all interconnected aspects of the career of public service that he embraced with such conviction.

The first memorialist is Ambassador Lucius B. Battle, president of the Middle East Institute. His career in the public service includes an ambassadorship to Egypt and two assistant secretaryships. From the standpoint of his subject, "The Old and the New World Order," of particular importance was his time as special assistant to the two Deans who were secretary of state, Dean Acheson and Dean Rusk.

AMBASSADOR BATTLE: It is a great pleasure for me to pay tribute at the Miller Center to which Fritz gave so much and which has continued to flourish under Ken Thompson. I am very happy to see my cherished Nolting friends again, all of whom I have known for so many years and with whom I have shared so many things.

There is a lot of talk these days about a new world order. Much of it is a bit vague. Some of it is too optimistic, like a search for nirvana. Much of it is equally too pessimistic and sounds like paradise mislaid or postponed, or perhaps even lost forever.

Nevertheless, we are emerging from an old order that all in all served us pretty well. It was a sort of stability built on instability. The reshaping of the world after World War II produced some structures that were imperfect in nature, but still, by the measures of these institutions, fairly elastic.

The 1940s turned out some pretty good stuff in terms of the world and our role in it. The United Nations today looks better than it has in years; NATO, the Marshall Plan, the Coal and Steel Community, and others offer lessons that help us as we grope for a new world order.

Fritz Nolting and I were "present at the creation," if I may steal a phrase from my late boss, Dean Acheson. Fresh from the military service, raring to save the world, he and I were in European Affairs together. We were both country desk officers: he for the

Friends of Ambassador Nolting

Netherlands and I for Canada—an ocean apart but very good viewing positions to see what was happening in the world.

After a few years of that, we moved up a bit to the fifth floor, which was where the brass sat in those days. I became assistant to Dean Acheson, and Fritz and Murat Williams were assistants to Freeman Matthews, who was better known as "Doc" by most people, and who was the equivalent of today's undersecretary for political affairs—in those days, deputy undersecretary. We had a pretty good vantage point and participated rather actively in what happened for the rest of that period.

In the late 1940s, with the new secretary of state, Dean Acheson in place and with Truman emerging, the real Truman era began, and we saw some dramatic things happen. The whole postwar period was beginning to take shape. The United Nations was forming, perhaps oversold a bit as a panacea to all the world's afflictions. The United States took the initiative to disarm, beginning right after the war. Isolationists were raising their voices, but interventionists were drowning them out.

A whole series of historic events were happening: the Truman Doctrine, aid to Greece and Turkey, NATO, and the Marshall Plan. Out of all of these developments came the eventual recovery of Europe and the ultimate end of the Cold War without another global conflict, which is what we tried to avoid from the beginning. It was also the first test of collective security—the police action in Korea—which had then and has now far-reaching implications.

Why was the era successful in shaping a world order in forms that were absolutely new to the American people? What is different today?

Truman and Acheson had many things going for them, and a number of forces were present that made much of the success possible. First, they had a clear enemy: Russia and communism; in addition, China and the Eastern bloc countries. There was also an international willingness and necessity on the part of the world to unite against a common threat and to work together for economic recovery.

Second, there was an acceptance and a welcoming of the need for innovation and new ideas, particularly in Japan and Western Europe. Money was available like nothing we had ever seen before—real, untapped, unspent American dollars, put up by the American people for the recovery of Western Europe and the rearming of America, which they had neither anticipated nor wanted.

There was also new American confidence in itself. We had won the war; we could now win the peace. These were all pretty important factors combining for truly courageous leadership by Truman and Acheson, leadership that we all followed and in which we were all participants.

Look at the situation today. What factors loom large and in the direction of what sort of new world order? There is no clear enemy; the Cold War is over. Eastern Europe has changed faster than anyone could imagine. There is once again the recognition of the necessity for innovation, this time in Russia and the Eastern bloc countries. A huge vacuum needs to be filled; but there is no money, and there is a growing negativism about foreign aid in our country.

We have just concluded a limited regional war, fought with international support and under U.N. sponsorship—beyond the fondest dreams that any of us had in the 1940s. These factors give us a clearer playing field on which to build than seemed the case even a few months ago.

In my opinion, the new world order must be built with a set of bricks and building blocks different from those with which we worked in the past. The order established in the 1940s was based on confrontational, largely political and military issues. But the end of the Cold War was essentially due to cornerstones in the economic field.

Superpower competition will not be the cornerstones of the new order. In fact, cooperation is more likely, as at the Geneva Conferences. The world order this time will be based on three large trading blocs. The largest will be the European Union, which has come into its own. The next will be the North American Alliance of the United States and Canada. Last will be the Pacific Rim: Japan, Korea (probably North and South, who seem to be making strides to get together again) China, Taiwan, and perhaps even Australia and New Zealand, both of which have strong ties to

Europe and the United States, but which still are very likely to belong to this last group. And there is GATT and NAFTA.

War will not disappear, but global war will be unlikely. Conflicts will be managed regionally if only regional interests are involved, but perhaps with international participation in situations where global interests are challenged. Regional conflicts, I think, will be heavily ethnic—witness what has happened in Yugoslavia and Eastern Europe.

Given the success of the Persian Gulf War as an international effort, we now have an excellent opportunity to return to global security through police actions mandated by the U.N. Security Council. This situation requires, I think, some reexamination of our own War Powers Act, insofar as it appears to be in conflict with our U.N. Participation Act. It also requires a reexamination of ourselves and our actions, particularly some of our little ventures like Grenada and Panama, which I don't think fit into this particular scheme very well.

We are closer than we have been at any point to the 1940s' dream of a collective police action, rather than one-on-one conflict. This seems to me a good time to reassess this whole situation.

A lasting new world order will not be easy to achieve. We may once again have to accept a temporary, shorter-term stability built on a degree of instability. But I expect improvements, and many of them will be drawn from the experiences of the postwar period.

I am happy to have been involved and to have shared so many experiences of those years with Fritz Nolting. He had the qualities the era demanded: creativity, dedication, integrity, and moral and ethical decency. Those were the forces that were needed for the post-World War II period. They are the same forces, I think, needed in building the new world order. I only wish that Fritz were here to help us.

NARRATOR: Our next speaker is Ambassador William E. Colby, counsel of Donovan, Leisure, Newton, and Irvine; first secretary of the American Embassy in Saigon; chief, Far Eastern division of the CIA; executive director, deputy director, and then director of Central Intelligence; and, most pertinent to his topic today, ambassador and director of Civil Operations and Rural Development Support in Saigon from 1968 to 1971.

AMBASSADOR COLBY: Very few people have fought a lonely struggle and apparently an unpopular one, only to be vindicated as was Fritz Nolting. When he arrived in Vietnam in 1961 he had no experience of Asia, but he wrapped that huge gangling frame of his into those tiny little chairs and intensely tried to understand the people of Vietnam—the leadership and the others. We had had some frictions in our relationships with Vietnam's somewhat prickly president, President Diem, and Fritz was instructed to set our relations on a positive and cooperative line.

He did become close to the leadership; he got to know the opposition; he got to know the people out in the countryside, where he traveled a great deal to understand that complex country. He was not naive about it. He did not see it as any perfect democracy. He recognized the mandarinate that it really was, as President Diem tried to modernize his country by the scruff of the neck and force it into the future. However, Fritz also realized that Diem did have an idea and a purpose, that the civilian opposition was of no particular significance and really represented the ancien régime (the colonial regime), and that the real problem was the rise of the Communist opposition in the form of a guerilla war.

It is amazing what the Communists now admit that they carefully concealed for so many years. They now admit that they began that war in 1959, two years before Fritz arrived. Thus, it was well on its way by the time he came along.

We had initially reacted by trying to build up the military forces to help defend South Vietnam against North Vietnam. Our mental image of the struggle was Korea, which had been a conventional soldier's war, but both the Vietnamese and Fritz, with his understanding, realized that this was a different kind of war. This was a people's war. It had to be fought at the village level, and that was the key—a political approach to the village. How do you energize the villagers to defend their country and their community against this onslaught from outside, particularly when some of the onslaught was inside, which made the problem even more complex?

But Fritz did understand, working with the government, recognizing that they had to be nationalist. They could not do our will, as Americans are wont to expect foreigners to do in every possible circumstance; they had to assert their nationalism if they were to contest the nationalist appeal that the enemy was offering to the population.

Working his way gradually through the problem in the best tradition of good diplomacy, Fritz brought the American government around to support a new approach toward the problem: a policy of strategic hamlets. It wasn't working very well; there was a lot of fakery in it. Some of the people didn't understand it. Some of it was expressed in much too theoretical terms. Nevertheless, Fritz deliberately kept at it and kept supporting it, and it began to work.

Accordingly, by the end of 1962, a Communist apologist, Wilfred Burchett, the Australian who had visited on the Communist side and had been supportive of the North Koreans and the North Vietnamese, said 1962 belonged to the government. In other words, the government had taken the initiative on a strategy with Fritz's full support and participation and was moving in the right direction.

There was an explosion in 1963, of course. We know it as the Buddhist explosion. Fritz again tried to work his way through the problems caused by the presentation of this kind of imagery to the American people—primarily in the form of a bonze burning himself in protest in a city square—and the problems of getting the increasingly exasperated Americans to continue a solid position of support of President Diem.

This development led to some rather major confrontations with very significant people in the United States government over whether we should stay with President Diem or get a new leader. In one of the more amazing feats of misperception that I can recall, no one ever suggested who the new leader would be.

In any case, we also have a historical perspective for the problems with the Buddhists in the somewhat similar fundamentalistic explosion we saw in Iran a few years later led by the Ayatollah. Quite frankly, the Buddhist leadership in Vietnam had many similarities to the Ayatollah's fundamentalism and antimodernism.

This struggle over whether we should stay with Diem or not continued into the Cabinet room of our President. Fritz made his position very, very clear; he got a lot of abuse from very senior people in the American government and from the press for his view that we should stay with Diem, that it was hard to work with him, but we should stay. The President gave the signals to the contrary. Fritz had to withdraw from the field, defeated on that issue. A rebellion in Vietnam, which was encouraged by the United States—no question about it—led to the death of President Diem. It was not a death intended by President Kennedy or anyone else, but the fact is, the sword was unleashed and the sword was used.

Fritz then had to take a backseat, as we saw the worst of his and my predictions came true: chaos. We had chaos, and then we had the huge war that followed it. President Johnson, who had been opposed to the policy and much more attuned to Fritz's view, took over, but by that time Diem was gone.

If you play with the might-have-beens of history, it seems to me that if we had stuck to President Diem, one of two results would have occurred and Fritz would have been totally vindicated. First, President Diem might have been able to suppress the Buddhists, get the strategic hamlet program back on track, and gradually tamp the war down over the next couple of years. The other possibility was that he would have failed, and he would have been defeated over the next couple of years. Either result would have been better for the entire globe than what actually happened. I think that is the justification for Fritz's farseeing, sensible approach to the problems of Vietnam.

I am glad to say that I shared those views with him. He was much more articulate than I, but I have tried to give him full honor in the various steps that he took in that time.

NARRATOR: Hal Ford is one of the most respected senior intelligence officers to serve in any intelligence body. He taught at Davidson College and Georgetown University and was a research scholar at St. Antony's College at Oxford. He is the author of a very important article that Ambassador Nolting asked him to send him when they were together shortly before Fritz's death, "Modern

Friends of Ambassador Nolting

Weapons and the Sino-Soviet Estrangement," which dates the beginning of that split in 1958.

The last forum that Fritz Nolting attended at the Miller Center was conducted by Hal Ford, and the two of them essentially dominated the forum, exchanging ideas that sometimes converged and sometimes diverged. At the end of the meeting, I remember Ambassador Nolting reminding Hal, "I hope you'll send me these materials," and Hal Ford did just that.

Respected by all who know him and have served with him, we are delighted to have Hal Ford with us today.

MR. FORD: I speak with a little diffidence on several scores. One is that I have been asked to talk about intelligence as a public service, but on my left is William Colby, someone who could speak with much more experience and authority than I.

The second source of diffidence is that I never had the pleasure of serving with Fritz Nolting. During the time that he was in Vietnam, I was one of his customers in the Office of National Estimates, where my seniors constituted the body making top-level analyses for the senior policymakers. I enjoyed my session here with Fritz very much. We later had lunch together. In semiretirement, on my own, I am a part-time historian with the CIA, and part of that job has been devoted to policy-making in Vietnam and what role intelligence played or didn't play. Fritz was able to give me a lot of fine insights, even in the course of a short luncheon.

Third, I am somewhat diffident because I recently had the nerve to testify to Congress against the confirmation of my good friend, Bob Gates. Many of you may disagree with my action; I hope you will accept my motives, which I thought were honorable. I felt I could take no other stand.

My fourth sense of diffidence is that I am guilty of an intelligence failure. I tried to find some apt quotations that have to do with ambassadors and diplomats, and most of the ones I could find were not very flattering. I guess I looked in the wrong place. As an example, one writer, John Hay, was himself an ambassador. As a young man, he was one of Abraham Lincoln's secretaries. Later he was ambassador to the Court of St. James and thereafter secretary of state. He wrote at one time, "There are three species of creatures who, when they seem coming, are going; when they seem going, they are coming. These are crabs, diplomats, and women."

He may have been a chauvinist; I don't intend to be, and I am not going to settle for any other of those bad quotations about diplomats. Nevertheless, I do want to pay homage to Fritz and to the ambassadors here, and to all of the ambassadors and diplomats that I have known and with whom I have served. I want to pay homage to them for the way in which they carry out their many wide-ranging responsibilities, which are much broader than I think most of us have appreciated until we have seen them up close: representing U.S. interests; dealing with sometimes querulous host governments; sitting on top of often querulous U.S. country teams; bailing out American businessmen; and suffering innumerable congressional delegations ("codels") and visiting firemen who come through.

I want to pay particular homage to Fritz and to his colleagues in the sense that they are intelligence officers as well. By intelligence, I do not mean clandestine activities, but simply that it is their own experience and observations of their host governments and the insights that we get from embassies that usually are our best single source about the toughest intelligence questions. The easy intelligence questions have to do with military hardware—there is a silo or there is not, there are so many tanks and they have this or that kind of gun. The difficult questions are the soft questions—intentions. What is Castro going to do tomorrow? Castro might not know yet. Is Gorbachev for real? Questions of politics, sociology, economics, and intentions—it is there that the insights of the reporting of Fritz and his colleagues over the years have made such a lasting contribution.

The question I am addressing here today is, "How intelligent is Intelligence?" By "Intelligence" I mean the CIA and the rest of the people in Washington called the intelligence community: State, Defense, and others who deal with this area.

To be truly intelligent, as I see it, intelligence must pass over four sets of hurdles. First, how good is the reporting from the field? How candid, how perceptive? What preconceptions lay behind it?

The second set of hurdles is in regard to what happens to the information it gets to the analysts in Washington—myself, my colleagues, the State Department, and others. What kind of preconceptions do we have? How good are the analysts? Do they present materials that are helpful to the senior policymakers, or is it just a lot of coordinated mush and a kind of Charlie Brown wishy-washy?

The third set of hurdles involves the question, what kind of interplay exists between the people who produce intelligence—and that would include Bill Gates as director of Central Intelligence—and the White House, the secretary of state, and the secretary of defense? What impact does it make? How good is the intelligence? What kind of market should it enjoy? What kind of preconceptions are present among the senior policymakers? How receptive are they to it? At times they are somewhat ignorant of what intelligence can do. Similarly, the intelligence people are somewhat ignorant at times of the many, many burdens and the numerous considerations that go into policy-making, not only as to the picture of the world, which intelligence hopes to find out, but also of the commitments that a president has at home and abroad, his concern—I hope someday her concern—for his position within the party and within the country. In short, how will this policy play in Peoria? These are considerations that the intelligence officers perhaps don't appreciate too well.

The fourth set of hurdles is embodied in the question, are intelligence and policy-making stuck to the patterns of the past, or are they receptive to the entirely new world of challenges that face us, which Ambassador Battle outlined so well. Our policy-making and intelligence structures were formed 45 years ago to face a world that is now different in many important respects.

It is my understanding that the government and intelligence are moving well to meet this new world, and I wish them well. More important, however, than what new priorities intelligence gives itself, more important than the thousands of computers that they are buying, and more important than the reorganization that they may make is what kind of people do they have. The answer is always in people.

I want to give credit once again to the people I have known and served with in the State Department and the Foreign Service, men and women who are well educated, well steeped in the subject matter of their assignments, who are acute observers who go where the evidence takes them, and who have the courage of their convictions and look on themselves as professionals, trying to discern the truth and promote the national interest in a world of often chaotic politics abroad and at home.

Thus, despite all of the hazards that intelligence faces and how intelligent intelligence is, you finally have to get down to a much broader definition of intelligence. Let me share a couple of definitions from the dictionaries. A short definition of intelligence is, "the faculty of understanding; the capacity to know or apprehend." A slightly longer one from another dictionary is, "the power of successfully meeting any situation, especially a novel situation by proper behavior adjustments; also the ability to apprehend the inner relationships of presented facts in such a way as to guide action towards a desired goal."

Hence, U.S. intelligence has a definite chance of becoming intelligent with a small *i* if the White House, the Congress, the director of Central Intelligence, and the U.S. intelligence community support and recruit intelligence and policy officers who embody these broadest definitions of intelligence and, on a continuing basis, demand the finest, the most honest, and the most candid performance from them—in short, the kind of performance that Fritz Nolting personified.

NARRATOR: Rhodes Scholar, reporter and assistant to the editor of the *Richmond News Leader*, Foreign Service officer beginning in 1947, initially first secretary in San Salvador, then ambassador to El Salvador from 1961 to 1964—Murat Williams brings us to the core of the family.*

---

*Murat passed away before we completed the volume.

Friends of Ambassador Nolting

MR. WILLIAMS: I am here because of a long relationship with Fritz. It goes back to the days when Fritz was my hero, something he remained for a long time. It is unusual in high school and college to find a hero among your fellow students. Fritz was a hero whom we worshipped, first in that schoolhouse in Richmond, where we had our heroes on the walls: General Lee, General Jackson, General Washington, and sometimes, Mr. Jefferson. Some light reflected from those pictures on the walls on Fritz, and some of us confused the qualities of Fritz with the qualities of those who were on the wall, all to the good.

The thing about Fritz is that he was a self-effacing person. He was also an extremely serious seeker after truth. The only time I ever saw him frustrated was when he and I were in a seminar course here at the University on the transcendentals of Aristotle. Our professor gave us the impression that he knew the subject matter. After six hours in the course, we all admitted to each other that we didn't have a clue as to what it was all about.

The fact that Fritz did so much in the Foreign Service was a great break for the Foreign Service. It added a sheen of honor to the Foreign Service to have a person like Fritz Nolting as one of its career officers. I know that people raised their opinion of the Foreign Service because Fritz was in it. That certainly was true among his hero worshippers in Virginia.

Fritz had a quality of self-effacement, which was in great contrast to the fact that diplomats began to seek celebrity status, a quality to which many of us objected among our diplomats in the years after the war. Fritz was never a celebrity diplomat. He never had any idea of getting public credit for what he was doing. He was only doing what he considered to be the right thing, in the best tradition of his Virginia antecedents and those heroes on the wall behind him.

I'm delighted that I was invited to join this worthy celebration of Fritz's character and achievements.

CHAPTER TWO

Kennedy, NATO, and Southeast Asia[*]

AMBASSADOR FREDERICK E. NOLTING

NARRATOR: By your record-breaking presence at the Miller Center, Ambassador Nolting, you have proven what I thought would be the case—there is little need for any introduction this morning. As a matter of fact, Frederick Nolting probably ought to introduce the Miller Center to you since he was so largely responsible for its beginnings, early history, furnishings, foundations, and all the other things that got us started.

Aside from a very distinguished military career, in which he rose from lieutenant junior grade to lieutenant commander in World War II, Ambassador Nolting's career may be divided into four parts: diplomat, banker, scholar, and educator. That of diplomat is the most central to our concerns here this morning. He spent 18 years in the Department of State, leaving with the permanent rank of minister. During that time he was concerned primarily with European and Far Eastern affairs. One of his functions was officer in charge of dealing with Swiss Benelux affairs.

---

[*]*Reprinted with permission from* The Kennedy Presidency: Seventeen Intimate Perspectives of John F. Kennedy. *Lanham, Md.: University Press of America, 1985.*

So if any of you have any Swiss bank accounts, today is the time to raise any questions you may have. He was alternate permanent representative to the North Atlantic Council. He became our deputy representative to NATO. He was concerned with the office of political affairs at NATO. He dealt also, in the 1950s, with Mutual Security Affairs as a special assistant to the secretary of state for Mutual Security Affairs. He was a member of the United States Delegation to the Sixth General Assembly. He served as coordinator of Far Eastern foreign assistance, and one could go on indefinitely. But in those 18 years he gained the respect of a great many people, some of whom are present today.

It took him less time to reform, improve, and strengthen the private sector and the economy. I counted 16 years but I may have missed a few years. He began with an investment firm, I think, in Richmond. He served there prior to World War II for five years. He then came back, after his distinguished career in the State Department and served as vice president in the European office of Morgan Guaranty in Paris and subsequently, assistant to the chairman of Morgan Guaranty in New York.

His major area of responsibility was in the Far East during a very critical and much discussed period in our history: the Vietnam War. His preparation for that centered primarily on his service in the government in both Far Eastern and European affairs. He served as ambassador to Vietnam from 1961 to 1963.

His role as educator began as a graduate student at the University of Virginia. He received not one but two master's degrees, one from Virginia and one from Harvard. He also received the Ph.D. degree from Virginia. He returned to the University of Virginia after his service in the private sector to become the first director of the Miller Center. It is appropriate that we now turn in our consideration of the Kennedy presidency to Ambassador Nolting. He will not only talk about the Vietnam period, but also about his other areas of responsibility at NATO, Mutual Security, and national defense, as they relate to the European area. It is a great privilege to have you with us.

AMBASSADOR NOLTING: Ken, you have a fabulous memory as well as a very generous nature. I can't begin this talk without

Ambassador Frederick E. Nolting

paying tribute to Ken Thompson's work here at the Miller Center. I know because I tried it for awhile. He has really made a national institution out of a small beginning, and I can't think of a greater contribution to the University of Virginia, and to the enlightened governance of our country, than what you have done at the Miller Center.

NARRATOR: Thank you. I had solid foundations on which to build.

AMBASSADOR NOLTING: My views of the Kennedy administration and its accomplishments in foreign policy do not coincide altogether with some of the previous speakers at these Forums. I was struck by a few things Arthur Schlesinger said. He spoke of the New Frontier's "addiction to activism" as "its besetting sin." I do not disagree so much with that, but I think it needs a great deal of qualification. He made no direct reference to Vietnam or to Southeast Asia. He did talk about the "fantasy of counterinsurgency." I simply raise a question about that, recalling the situation confronting the United States at that time. Khrushchev and the Russian government had made it clear that their attack on the free world would come through wars of "national liberation," as Khrushchev termed them, not through a major confrontation with the West. We were afraid of that. Counterinsurgency was one of the options that was available and useful in the defense of the free world, if wisely used, as the British did in Malaya.

These are a few more observations: Dean Rusk, in his contribution, makes no mention of Southeast Asia in the early 1960s. He makes no mention of Vietnam until he speaks of the drying up of grass-roots support for the war effort in 1966. He makes no mention whatsoever of the United States' role in the 1960s, particularly in 1963, in the overthrow of the government of South Vietnam. Something ought to be on the record about that—not just a gap in the history of this period.

Ted Sorensen, a close friend of President Kennedy, did make one reference to Vietnam saying: "We didn't give enough attention to Southeast Asia and Vietnam in particular." Well, that's the understatement of the year. There was every effort made to try to bring the State Department, in particular, and the White House into the Vietnam issue early on. It started before my day and it continued until President Kennedy's death. By that time, we were so deeply involved in bailing out the military junta that the United States had helped put into power that President Johnson thought there was no way out, except through the use of a great number of American combat forces. Sorensen also said that the Laotian settlement of 1962 was a great diplomatic triumph. Well, if that was a triumph of diplomacy, I don't know the meaning of the word. Averell Harriman was the negotiator. He told me that he was under instructions from President Kennedy to get a settlement of the Laotian question at any cost. In the early days of the Kennedy administration, President Kennedy went on television and said we were going to take a stand in Laos. Those of you who know the inaccessibility of Laos can understand how horrified the Joint Chiefs of Staff were to hear that the President had decided to make a stand in Laos. There wasn't any way to get in there except by air, and that didn't make much sense. So the President backed off of that idea and decided Vietnam was the place to make the stand. But then, as if in order to open up the flank of Vietnam, he ordered the Laotian settlement. This treaty definitely weakened, both physically and from the point of view of morale, the chances of the successful defense of South Vietnam.

One other remark about Sorensen: He thought the Cuban missile crisis was a very great American success. I agree with that, in part. It was handled better than anything I know of in the tragically short administration of President Kennedy. It was successful in avoiding nuclear war. Nevertheless, the fact that the United States was successful in getting the Russians to back away from the installation of missiles in Cuba was only to come back to where we were before the Bay of Pigs. It is not, it seems to me, proportionate to talk in terms of a big success without mentioning the previous big disaster.

I am trying to fill in some gaps in this oral history. One must keep in mind, however, that my view is only one of many. I think one always finds that there is a difference between the viewpoint of those in the field abroad and those who serve in the inner circles in

Ambassador Frederick E. Nolting

Washington. Certainly I was not one of the inner-circle people in Kennedy's administration.

This leads me to what I'd like to say first about Kennedy and our European allies in NATO. I was in NATO for several months during the Kennedy administration and for about five years under the Eisenhower administration. The difference between those two administrations with respect to our European allies was very great. I have no doubt in my mind that the NATO system of this great North Atlantic alliance functioned much better under Eisenhower than it did under Kennedy. There are several reasons for this. General Eisenhower was known and respected. He was tried and true from the point of view of the NATO countries. His record as supreme commander helped, as well as his willingness to consult and consider—in terms of U.S. policy—the views of our NATO allies. President Kennedy was not inclined in that way from the perspective of the NATO countries. Our European allies were attracted by his freshness, his dynamism, his personal attraction, and his oratory. But they felt that he was untried; he was less willing to consult; he was less reliable as an ally from the European perspective. For example, some of our allies were alarmed by his earlier speeches in the Senate in which he went all out for self-determination of European colonies, particularly those in Africa. While the idea of self-determination was generally acceptable to most of the colonial powers in NATO, they didn't want it to happen overnight. They had to have some preparation time.

Another point I would like to make is that the NATO allies did not feel that Secretary Rusk was as close to or had as much influence with Kennedy as John Foster Dulles had with Eisenhower or Dean Acheson had with Truman. They felt a certain reserve and distance there. Perhaps that was overcome in later years, but this was, I think, the prevailing perspective from NATO in the first year of the Kennedy administration. There was no consultation in NATO whatsoever under the Kennedy administration on the Southeast Asian problem. While the French had set a not very good precedent on this, the United States had argued for years—and I was on the Political Consultation Committee—the benefits to be derived from constant consultation on political problems, however thorny they might be. To have our government, because we had a hot potato, refuse to talk about it, was not good diplomacy or statesmanship.

As we all know, no president ever has a clean slate on which to write, not even George Washington, and certainly no modern president. Therefore, one has to think about continuity and distribute responsibilities, praise, and criticism in accordance with the flow of history and the dynamics of the process of ruling any country. Just as Kennedy inherited from Eisenhower the makings of the disaster of the Bay of Pigs, so Johnson inherited from Kennedy the makings of the disaster of Vietnam. It is very difficult, however, to say where these things could have been halted or where they could have been changed.

My thesis is that the great error of the Kennedy administration was its misunderstanding of the issues involved in Vietnam in the 1960s and its reaction to those issues. More specifically, the error was in its refusal to understand that the elected constitutional government of Vietnam was the best available. If we were to help South Vietnam survive at all, the only available vehicle that could sustain and carry forward the country was the government that had been in power eight years (after two elections) and that had run into a great deal of Communist-inspired trouble. Now, this change of U.S. position came about, from my point of view, rather suddenly. In 1961 and 1962, our efforts to help South Vietnam through its duly elected government were for the most part successful. The testimony on that comes not only from Washington, but other capitals, including especially France. This may surprise you, because France had a chip on its shoulder about Americans taking over its responsibilities in helping South Vietnam. But Couve de Murville, for example, told me on two occasions that the American effort in 1961 and 1962 in South Vietnam was succeeding from the point of view of the French interests still there, and they were considerable. The Michelin Rubber Company, the major banks, and the major shipping companies were all saying, "Keep it up; the country is beginning to get pacified; it is beginning to work."

When we first arrived with our families, we could hardly go out of Saigon without an escort, and then you took a chance on getting ambushed. By 1962 we could drive to many provinces without escort and without much danger. You would have threats of assassinations and bombings and so forth, but our children went to school there and we lived a normal life. This was just one indication of the gradual pacification brought about by the Diem government with our help and advice.

It was true that the Kennedy administration had stepped up the amount of aid from the Eisenhower level of about $150 million a year to, until 1963, about $350 million a year. I remember that figure well because every morning going to the office I would say, "My God, what am I going to do with this million dollars today to make it worth it to the American people?" And I certainly don't claim that we succeeded every day or even every other day. But on the whole, it was getting better. Even Ho Chi Minh testified that 1962 was Diem's year. He gave this to Wilfred Burchett, an Australian correspondent of Communist leanings, who spent most of his time either in Hanoi or with the Communist Viet Cong in South Vietnam. His testimony, I thought, was significant. He said not only that 1962 was Diem's year, but after the overthrow of Diem's government in 1963, he quoted one of the Communist leaders as saying they could not imagine that the United States would be so stupid as to preside over the overthrow of the only government that had any standing and status in South Vietnam. Why did we do this?

The Buddhist crisis is generally regarded as the releasing cause. There was, however, more to it than that. This comes back directly to the Kennedy administration. It was the impatience of the gung-ho boys; it was the 1964 election coming up; it was the desire of President Kennedy to make up for the bullying he got from Khrushchev in Vienna in the first meeting; it was the Berlin Wall, which was a slap in the face and which we didn't do much about—except for Kennedy's famous speech, "Ich bin ein Berliner." That didn't take one stone out of the Berlin Wall; it was perhaps encouraging to the West Berliners, but to my mind, it wasn't any great diplomatic stroke. On Vietnam in 1963 the influences upon Kennedy were divided. The State Department, my own department, took the lead in advocating such great pressures upon President Diem as to make it impossible for him to govern. This pressure was reciprocal in the sense that the more pressure there was from Washington, the more the Buddhist agitators put pressure on our press, and through our press on Washington, to get rid of the Diem government.

Another thing that was absolutely clear, which we reported countless times, was that the number one objective of the Viet Cong was the overthrow of the Diem government. That was the identical objective of the radical wing of the Buddhist government. This radical wing did not represent the Buddhist population by any means. It was a new organization founded only the year before. There never had been a hierarchical organization of Buddhists in Vietnam. Each bonze had his own village to look after and his own marriages and burials to perform, but he wasn't responsible to the next guy on the totem pole. There wasn't any overall Buddhist organization. So, this was a new thing that was formed for a political purpose, and it achieved that political purpose. While I have no proof of this except circumstantial evidence, I firmly believe that it was infiltrated and controlled by the Viet Cong through Hanoi. I think the misunderstandings of our government with respect to that fact was one of the biggest contributing factors to our change of policy.

In the 1950s, almost every year someone would come up with a story about NATO in "disarray." Compared to the Kennedy administration in 1963 on the issue of Southeast Asia, NATO's disarray was nothing. You could sit around the NATO council table and settle issues with the representatives of 15 nations much more readily and reasonably than you could with the representatives of the various departments and agencies in Washington in 1963. This was so much so that President Kennedy himself at one meeting in 1963 said, "My government has gone completely to pieces. Who is right? Who has the information? What shall I do?" Unfortunately, Averell Harriman took the bit in his teeth and ran off with the show.

He wasn't any older than I am now and I don't see how anyone could have been so vindictive, authoritarian, and bullying as he was of everyone, including the President of the United States. His hatred of the Diem regime became greater and greater. It originated with President Diem's reluctance to sign the Laotian agreement that Harriman had negotiated. There was a personal friction between them on that. I had the job of persuading Diem to sign because there was very little else he could do. Harriman was out there in 1962 and threatened to cut off all American aid if he didn't. This involved not only Vietnamese objections to the treaty, which had no safeguards, but the Thais objected to it just as strongly as the Vietnamese did. But this started a personal distrust that certainly made it much more difficult to get any reasonable exchange of views in the National Security Council meetings that followed in the fall of 1963. It was very, very difficult.

Another factor was that President Kennedy had appointed Henry Cabot Lodge as the new ambassador to Saigon. Lodge and Harriman had, I think, agreed beforehand that the only thing to do was to encourage the dissident generals to revolt, to take over. Lodge was pulling from the Saigon end for this while Harriman was pushing from the Washington end. Some of the rest of us were trying to stand in the way to hold the fort, so to speak, but to no avail. Again, politics came into it very strongly for the reason that there were two very distinguished pillars of both parties—Lodge, whom I thought of as a piece of Republican asbestos to keep the heat off of Kennedy, and Harriman, who still had a lot of the political force of the Roosevelt heritage.

Now the young president was caught in a dilemma; there was no question about it. There were several things he could have done, but the worst alternative was what he opted to do. Even worse than the practical consequences of the coup were the moral effects. I will not go into the sequence of events here because I believe it is now clear that after the revolution things went from bad to worse, regardless of the number of troops that we put in and regardless of the fact that the cost went up dramatically: 57,000 American lives, eight years of dissension in our country, huge increases in public debt, and the inflation that afflicted us throughout the 1970s. The actions of the Kennedy administration set the stage for all this.

There is just one point I would like to make. You have developed, Ken, in your books a theme that appeals to me a very great deal: the role of morality and ethical dealings in foreign policy. Even worse than the practical results in Vietnam were the moral consequences. Diem's was a government to whom our president had personally promised noninterference in its internal affairs. Just before I left Saigon in August 1963, President Diem asked me whether this change of ambassadors meant any change in U.S. policy. I said, "No, I'm assured, Mr. President, that it doesn't," and he said, "Well, would you just check that for me?" I sent a special telegram to what was called the highest levels and got one back from "the highest levels"—that's supposed to be the president, although you never know for sure—saying, "No change in policy and you can tell him that straight out." So, I took the telegram and translated it for him. While it was in my hand he said, "Mr. Ambassador, I believe you, but I'm afraid your information is incorrect." He was quite right, because by the time I got back to Washington this thing was out of hand and there was nothing we could devise to stop it. I want to say that the denials that were made after the coup in November, that our government had nothing to do with it, were too much for me to take. I don't think that anyone ought to try to cover up something of that sort when it is, in the first place, immoral and deceitful, and in the second place, impossible.

QUESTION: I can't remember whether the domino theory antedated Mr. Kennedy's presidency or not, but it certainly was in its ascendancy during his term and later, as Vietnam became more difficult. It has always intrigued me that there hasn't been a fair analysis of the working of that theory in the 20-20 gaze of hindsight. Indonesia, for example, is a country that had all the marks, under Sukarno, of heading into the Communist camp. It did not happen, however, even though they had a great massacre that, perhaps, contributed to its prevention. With your perspective, I would like for you to comment on the domino theory. Was it viable in the beginning? Did it have any continued aspects that are defensible today?

AMBASSADOR NOLTING: Yes, I think so, Leigh. If it's taken literally, as one domino falling right after another, one knocking the other one over, that, of course, is not what was meant. The cumulative effect of Communist victories are very great. Kampuchea (Cambodia) is certainly one example now in that area. So is Laos. Of course, it didn't go as far as Malaya. That was stopped by the British before they got out. But I think there is a certain momentum that builds up. In the case of Vietnam, it has been argued that through enormous sacrifices that effect was held up, to a certain extent, for eight years and that this gave other countries a chance to strengthen their resistance. To what extent that is true, I'm not sure. But I do think, in general, the domino theory, while an oversimplification, has a certain basis in fact.

QUESTION: Mr. Ambassador, had the Kennedy administration retained support for the Diem regime, and had the administration, the secretary of defense, and the Joint Chiefs decided to take decisive action and support within the first two or three years of the buildup of the Communist effort, before North Vietnam really came into it, could we have succeeded in keeping South Vietnam a free country?

AMBASSADOR NOLTING: Do you mean after the revolution or before?

QUESTION: If they had retained support for President Diem's regime and the military had made a decisive decision.

AMBASSADOR NOLTING: My opinion is that the answer is yes. With our continued support of the legitimate government, which was gaining ground on Ho Chi Minh, I think that with continued American support, there was a chance of coming out with a fairly stable solution—a divided Vietnam, somewhat in the pattern of Korea or Germany, which is certainly not a very satisfactory solution, but one we have had to settle for in several cases. The chances of that happening, followed by gradually getting the two halves of Vietnam together through trade and other means, would have been good—and that without American combat forces.

I might make one other remark which is apropos of the domino theory. I think one of the conceptual errors of the Kennedy administration early on was to think about the three states of Indochina—the old French Indochina—as separate entities. They are racially separate, but they had been grouped together a long time under the French empire. As a strategic area, the Communists always thought about it as one area. It didn't make any difference to them which side of the Laotian or Cambodian border they were on. They thought about it as one area, including North Vietnam, South Vietnam, Laos, and Cambodia. Because we weren't sufficiently educated on that part of the world, myself included, we looked at the countries separately; we thought they could be defended separately. That was a big conceptual error on the part of the United States.

QUESTION: Ambassador Nolting, may I say something? I was in the Joint Staff at that time writing papers in this particular area. There were two teams of us writing papers in this area and for one thing, we weren't allowed to do anything to try to win the war. That was a rule set down. And, for another, when we would try to look at it as a whole area, it would be split up for us when it went across the river. There were two ways to stop things at that point. Both involved moving the war supplies out of China, down into South Vietnam through Laos, and through North Vietnam itself. And the Chief's staff proposed to close off the port, Haiphong, Hanoi, and to close the valley coming down from China, which was very narrow and could have been closed with one explosion. This was in the early 1960s during the secret war in Laos, the top secret war in Laos.

AMBASSADOR NOLTING: Very interesting.

COMMENT: They called it Cochin China historically and changed it to Indochina under the French, and we lost the threads of the strategic implication of that early on. We had a mental block about Indochina being part of the empire of France. I can remember when it was a single, strategic entity, Cochin China.

COMMENT: I just wanted to say how much I endorse what Ambassador Nolting has said. I suppose professional diplomacy moves different minds in the same direction. This is so very much how I see it. I just wanted to put that on record. And I also wanted to make two other endorsing remarks. One is about the attitude of the European allies toward the Kennedy administration. I think there was in Europe admiration and affection for Kennedy as a bright young person—something new. There is no doubt, I think, that the European governments were more unhappy with the Kennedy administration than with any other administration since the war. We only had two years of Kennedy, but certainly those two years produced a deep malaise and unhappiness in European governments. I think there is no doubt about that.

The second thing I wanted to say was about Cuba. I was the British ambassador in Cuba during those years. I think there is no doubt that the Russians—this I owe really to Fidel among other people—always had two options. If they could get away with having missiles in Cuba, well and good. That would have compensated for the river of money they were pouring into Cuba because Cuba, on the whole, has not been such a success for the Russians. And if they didn't, they could always retire. I think when one is talking about U.S. policy toward Cuba, I don't know that getting Russians to accept their plan B instead of their plan A was such victory, for the Bay of Pigs operation was a setback all over Central America. In other words, I agree with Ambassador Nolting's judgment that although the negotiation was brilliantly handled by the Kennedy brothers, it didn't really get the United States back to square one.

AMBASSADOR NOLTING: There is also the fact that as a part of the secret deal, NATO's southern flank was badly affected by our agreement to withdraw our missiles from Turkey. Ever since there has been this weakness in the southern flank of NATO.

COMMENT: And Turkey protects the Middle East; it protects Israel.

AMBASSADOR NOLTING: This was part of the deal that was not made public—the removal of the missiles from Turkey. I'm not sure that we came further than halfway back on the deal. I'm glad to hear your testimony as British ambassador in Cuba that you feel that too.

COMMENT: Yes, I do, a lot.

NARRATOR: You wouldn't want to say whether it was also the policy of your government, at the time of the coup, to be as critical of what was being done as Ambassador Nolting is.

COMMENT: Well, this was the high-water mark of nonconsultation with your allies, the Vietnam opposition. I remember Prime Minister Harold Wilson laying down instructions that were sent to British ambassadors in various places saying: "This is Harold Wilson. Our attitude is no public criticism of our American allies whatever they do." To send out the word publicly like that clearly meant that we were unhappy. Kennedy, however, gave little attention to this.

It does seem to me that the ignorance of your policy outside France about Vietnam is appalling. I also think that most of the time the European allies didn't really know what they were talking about. They had quite good ambassadors on the spot, but I don't think the government or the press or the Parliament of a country like Britain, or a country like Germany, really knew what was going on in Vietnam. Therefore, I'm not sure that our judgments are really all that valid.

AMBASSADOR NOLTING: With the exception of the Bob Thompson mission—the British mission under Sir Robert Thompson. That was successful counterinsurgency, the very thing that was criticized by some of the speakers here.

COMMENT: Yes, and the very thing that's criticized in Central America.

COMMENT: I'm going to come back to nonconsultation. I was intrigued by your remark that the Kennedy administration did not consult with the European allies about the involvement in Southeast Asia. I wondered if perhaps that might be attributed, in part, to American sensitivity about getting involved.

AMBASSADOR NOLTING: Yes, but I don't think our allies in NATO would have viewed it that way. To my mind, it was just because we had a very difficult problem that we didn't want to talk about, just as the French didn't want to talk about Algeria (although that was a different thing because Algeria was a province of France). But Vietnam was something that we wanted to do on the side, do it ourselves, and didn't want anybody else to tell us how, I suppose. At least, that was Washington's view at the time.

QUESTION: Did you have a say outside the NATO treaty area?

AMBASSADOR NOLTING: Yes, indeed. That is an important point.

One point I keep coming back to in my mind is that the general interpretation of America's getting a thumb in the wringer in Vietnam, then our hand, then our arm, is not true. I don't think it was true under Eisenhower and I don't think it was true under Kennedy up until his last tragic months. I think that the U.S. support of the coup was a political decision of crucial importance. It was opposed by the CIA. I should make this very clear because anytime anything like that happens, everyone says, "Oh, the dirty CIA did it." The CIA was then under John McCone and Pat Carter and they were absolutely opposed. All the "tea leaves" (intelligence reports) in each of the NSC meetings said, "No, don't do it, you'll get into a worse fix. Don't support the military junta. They are no good." That was my view also. That was, ironically enough, President Johnson's view.

I remember that after one of the meetings Johnson, who was then vice president, said: "Keep it up, you fellows arguing against this change, this foolish move, keep it up." I remember saying after one of those remarks, "Mr. Vice President, you carry an awful lot of weight and you can see that we are beleaguered here and we could use some help." Vice President Johnson said, "President Kennedy has invited me to attend these NSC meetings on the condition that I do not express an opinion."

QUESTION: Mr. Ambassador, you put a finger on something I want to emphasize. Each of these presidencies inherit the continuation, not in isolation. They don't get a clean slate. You talked about plan A and plan B of the Russians. Well, they have got plan A and plan B any place that they want to move: Ethiopia,

Somalia, Laos, Cambodia. So, I would like you to take it one step further in your conversation. In Malaysia you did something about it. How would you apply that case to the present and future?

AMBASSADOR NOLTING: I don't think that you can draw specific analogies or parallels between the South Vietnam case and the case in Central America or anywhere else. I think you should, and our government does of course, have plans and alternative plans for almost every eventuality. When to put them into action and when not to is really the crucial question I think that you raised. My instinct is one of extreme caution in moving in to take or to manipulate power in other governments. But that doesn't rule out doing it when you have to. It is a question of judgment. In the case of Vietnam I think the judgment was very bad. I think it is generally bad when we try to move in on internal situations. I don't think this is a very good analogy, but perhaps the Middle East would be a lot better if we hadn't interfered with the Shah.

QUESTION: Would you say Southeast Asia would be a whole lot better if President Marcos is not overthrown with American aid?

AMBASSADOR NOLTING: With American aid, yes. If the Filipinos overthrow him, that's not our responsibility. We don't get involved in the same sense that we got involved in the overthrow in Vietnam.

COMMENT: Or the Shah.

AMBASSADOR NOLTING: I'm not so well-informed about the Shah and I don't think it's an exact analogy by any means. But it seems to me that, more times than not, when we move in on something of that sort, we do it wrong.

QUESTION: In early 1963 I was in Vietnam as a member of a group coming from the Pentagon. There was talk to this group that they were about to launch a national liberation campaign, everything looked good, there was going to be an effective victory on the side of South Vietnam. And, of course, events proceeded on and you

Ambassador Frederick E. Nolting

have alluded to some of the mistakes as you saw them. I have since read the comment that the reason we ultimately lost in South Vietnam was because the North Vietnamese were more willing to die for their cause than the South Vietnamese were for their cause. The reason for this was that the South Vietnamese saw us as being the government of South Vietnam. Furthermore, the Asia for the Asians' aspect of Ho Chi Minh's cause was such that, in effect, we were precluded from ever being able to achieve success because it was too much our government, too much our control of the affairs in South Vietnam. I wonder if you would comment on that.

AMBASSADOR NOLTING: I think we were always under that handicap from the year 1954 on, but nowhere near as much as after taking the responsibility for a new revolutionary government. President Diem's greatest fear—or vulnerability—was being called an American puppet, from which the Viet Cong would profit. That is one of the reasons we had such a hard time with the press. They wanted the Americans to claim everything good that happened as an American victory, while we tried to hide it under a bushel saying, "No, this is a Vietnamese government action," whether it was the building of a new school, the opening of a hospital, the land reform, the increase to three rice crops a year in the delta through hybrid seed, or the increase in education. We tried not to make it seem an American achievement, which was very hard for our press to take. They thought this was a concession to the Vietnamese government that we shouldn't be making. They wanted us to be nationalistic—not helpers but bosses.

I don't think the North Vietnamese were any braver. They had a cause that was more clear-cut, in a sense, because of foreign aid to the south. Of course, Russian and Chinese aid in large quantities to the Viet Cong was not made public. I think this advantage was vastly increased by the coup. In fact, the political base of South Vietnamese nationalism was removed and destroyed with the overthrow of the Diem government in 1963. This was the major reason why the military governments that succeeded it were so unsuccessful.

QUESTION: When McGeorge Bundy spoke here, he described Mr. Harriman as quite a strong force in the Washington group. What would have been the relationship? Would Bundy have been a junior partner, you might say, or some such relationship, with Harriman performing a sort of ministerial role? Rusk or McNamara were probably not nearly on top of this thing. I'm trying to think of the group that was pushing for the overthrow of President Diem.

AMBASSADOR NOLTING: Mike Forrestal, who was young in those days, was brought into the White House staff under Bundy, and President Kennedy said, "You keep an eye on Averell Harriman. You are my eyes and ears on Averell Harriman." It was like trying to tie up a stallion with a piece of string—he couldn't do it. Furthermore, instead of Forrestal keeping an eye on Harriman, he became Harriman's man. He was one of those who was pushing in the White House for a change, an overthrow.

McGeorge Bundy was equivocal on the subject, in my opinion. Our friend Dean Rusk was also. George Ball was in Harriman's camp and so was the assistant secretary for Far Eastern Affairs, Roger Hilsman. The majority of the military, the Joint Chiefs of Staff, certainly the CIA, Maxwell Taylor, and I and a few others were very much opposed. It would be interesting, if you get Bob McNamara down here, to quiz him a little on this subject.

QUESTION: What have we learned, if anything, about the possibilities of negotiating settlements? As you know, much of the literature now speaks of missed opportunities for negotiating settlements in Vietnam. I really have two points here, the latter of which you may not wish to put on the record. The first is, were there any pursuable conditions under which a negotiated settlement that would serve our interests could have been accomplished? Second, did Averell Harriman really think that would work in Laos, or was this seen as a domestic political ploy?

AMBASSADOR NOLTING: Let me take your last question first because it was chronologically first, in a way. I think Averell Harriman did, really and truly, think that the Russians were going to police the Laotian treaty—he used the word to me—and make the others tow the line. That meant the U.S.S.R. would make the North Vietnamese take out the 40,000 troops who were in Laos, making the Ho Chi Minh trail into what Joe Alsop later called "the Harriman Memorial Highway"; that they would let the Souvanna Pouma government into the territories controlled by the Pathet Lao, the Communist Laotians; that they would make a real effort to have this tiny country taken out of the area of conflict, thereby blocking off a good part of the Ho Chi Minh trail and the supply routes from North Vietnam and China. I think Harriman really believed this. I think it was naive. He told me he had a "fingertips feeling," which I couldn't dispute successfully because he had been to Russia as ambassador. I said that my fingertips told me just the reverse.

On the other question about the chance for a negotiated settlement, I think there were several opportunities. One of them that came up—this came recently into play in the State Department history—was whether or not Nhu's reported talks with the Vietcong and representatives from Hanoi could have led to a negotiated settlement. Well, that was reported after I had been recalled. I never believed that Nhu was selling out his brother or his government. But I do think that, in desperation, he was probably trying to work out a negotiation that would have let South Vietnam continue to be independent, possibly with certain concessions to the North. I think that was one opportunity. Early on there were many, but that's the most recent.

NARRATOR: Before wishing you all a Merry Christmas, I would remind you that in the session just before Christmas we have followed the practice of having a speaker from the Miller Center family. Fritz Nolting remains part of that family. We are pleased he could be with us this morning for his important presentation. Thank you very much.

CHAPTER THREE

A Personal Appreciation: The Beginnings of a Revisionist View on Frederick Nolting

KENNETH W. THOMPSON

My first glimpse of Fritz Nolting on my arrival in Charlottesville was at a party. He and a couple of what I considered hard-line allies cornered me, apparently to test my thinking about foreign policy. As I remember it, the discussion was on Vietnam and how we could have won the war. I didn't disagree with much that was said, but I was resentful about having been overpowered. In the best academic tradition, I quickly constructed a stereotype of Fritz Nolting and lay in wait for a time that I might ambush him alone without any of his friends.

Part of my stereotype of Ambassador Nolting didn't last long. Fritz and Lindsay gave some of the best dinner parties in town. At Christmas they gathered four or five couples around the piano to sing Christmas carols. He asked my wife Beverly to be the accompanist. Other parties followed with the Dumas Malones as guests of honor on one occasion and the George McGhees on another. None of that was very hard-line.

When I was appointed to succeed him at the Miller Center, he let me know, smiling down from the stage at a fall convocation, that it was all right. I'd do. I had caught a whiff of his goodwill when the Noltings and the Jim Bears, who were hosts one autumn evening at a candlelight board dinner at Monticello, had included the Thompsons. Even though he was for victory in Vietnam, he couldn't be all bad, I thought. We still remember the good conversation and the beauty of Monticello in candlelight.

I could go on in this vein, admittedly satirical. It took time for me to learn all there was to know about Fritz Nolting, and I'm still learning. He wasn't at all the figure Averell Harriman had painted, nor the diplomat that banker George Ball once described. I started to understand that Fritz had to make a point. He wasn't just being stubborn in speaking out for Diem. It wasn't so much victory in Vietnam but political and cultural reality in which Diem was the best choice as leader among a collection of bad alternatives. He was a patriot for whom Vietnam's independence was most important. Near the end of his life, he was more prepared to live with some kind of a negotiated settlement and division of the country with Ho Chi Minh than accept the presumptuous terms that Harriman, Lodge, and even Kennedy sought to impose on South Vietnam as a condition of U.S. support. Fritz had traveled the countryside and knew that Diem had greater support than the generals who were seen as belonging to the ancien regime and as remnants of French colonialism. He also knew that Diem met the mandarin image that rural people especially understood. Finally, Fritz was convinced from his travels that conditions were improving and that at worst South Vietnam could hold its own and preserve independence and order, whatever might happen in the North. There would be peace based on conditions on the ground.

At the University of Virginia, Ambassador Nolting was a positive force. He had two master's degrees and a doctorate degree. He gave graduate courses both in the Department of Government and Foreign Affairs and the Darden School of Business. Law students attended some of his classes, including a seminar on ethics. Several times I overheard students in restaurants or coffeehouses debating one another on arguments Professor Nolting had made. Antiwar students were often critical. They saw Nolting as a defender of continuing the war. Pro-war students thought they had a friend. Over time, each was surprised to find that Nolting was against a gung ho attitude and large-scale American-led counterinsurgency in Vietnam. He knew the price of saturating the rural areas with American soldiers. Fritz sent his children to Vietnamese schools, and he tried to keep channels open to the people, including the opposition and the Buddhists.

Fritz maintained what amounted to daily contacts with President Diem. By contrast, his successor, Henry Cabot Lodge, rejected presidential orders on seven occasions from Kennedy and his superiors to explore whether or not any basis for negotiation existed. He rejected all seven orders to the point where one historian called him "the Raj." Lodge's idea was that the Vietnamese should come to him. Nolting went out among the Vietnamese and retained the trust of President Diem.

Through disappointment and, more recently, partial vindication, Ambassador Nolting comported himself with dignity, courtesy, and professionalism. From 18 years in the State Department, he knew the business of a diplomat. He combined the bottom-line mentality on new ventures in foreign policy with firmness on the basics and looked for outcomes rather than simple answers. His laugh turned grim situations into willingness to talk. He exchanged blow for blow with the whole Kennedy entourage (see chapter 2). In the end, however, he was outnumbered and outconspired. A longtime friend who was left in charge when he took leave from his post in Vietnam sold their friendship for a bowl of pottage and increased portion of prestige. Yet Fritz and his family retained their self-respect. They had no need to apologize for the generals' coup, whereas Harriman later admitted he was wrong. Some of us carried Fritz's flag-draped coffin down a hill to a country cemetery. We were proud then that we had known him. As history's scroll unfolds, we are prouder still.

II.

ADMINISTRATION AND GOVERNANCE

Professor Frederick C. Mosher

CHAPTER FOUR

The Legacy of Frederick C. Mosher[*]

Max O. Stephenson, Jr. and Jeremy F. Plant

Public Administration lost one of its most respected and consistently thoughtful scholars at the death of Frederick Camp Mosher on 21 May 1990. Over the course of a career that spanned five decades, "Fritz" Mosher—as he came to be known to his friends, colleagues, and acquaintances—authored or coauthored 15 books and dozens of articles; directed the operations of two major national government task forces; edited the *Public Administration Review* from 1953 to 1956; and served with distinction at four prestigious universities (Syracuse University, University of Bologna, University of California at Berkeley, University of Virginia) as well as in professional organizations such as the National Academy of Public Administration (NAPA) and the American Society for Public Administration (ASPA).

These intellectual contributions notwithstanding, Frederick Mosher's career is not fully encompassed by such a listing. His own

---

[*]*Reprinted with permission from* Public Administration Review *(March/April 1991, vol. 51, no. 2)* © *by the American Society for Public Administration (ASPA), 1120 G Street NW, Suite 700, Washington, DC 20005. All rights reserved.*

experience as a practitioner must also be examined. Mosher combined his distinguished efforts in academe with service to the Army Air Force, the Tennessee Valley Authority, the City of Los Angeles, the U.S. Department of State, and the United Nations. His experience as a professional was both wide and deep. That "real world" perspective profoundly influenced his analytic work throughout his life. In addition, as a scholar, Mosher appeared actively to seek out opportunities that allowed him to study government and its problems close-up. The frequent result of that intense interest in thoughtfully evaluating actual governmental practice was both sound scholarship *and* findings or observations of practical significance or relevance. Mosher was perhaps the quintessential "practitioner scholar."

Any essay seeking to analyze his career or even selections of his works, must be premised upon an important measure of humility. Mosher's scholarly corpus, his professional stature, and his many well-known contributions to the field together make an examination of his writings and career a challenging prospect. This article cannot (and does not) pretend to capture all of the subtlety and nuance of a glittering intellect. Instead, it begins modestly what will certainly be a sustained effort to assess more comprehensively his contributions to the discipline. This essay serves that larger purpose by offering an analytic overview of central concerns in what might be dubbed Mosher's intellectual journey. . . .

ORIENTATIONS

At least one fundamental issue underpinned the body of Mosher's writings. Mosher returned to that central theme via a systematic—if not always self-conscious—exploration of three major subthemes or areas of interest at various points in his career. The most significant overarching theme was his continuing attempt to address carefully, if not to resolve, a central tension implicit in the original tenets of the field of public administration. Those who founded the field did so on the basis of ultimately conflicting intellectual premises. Civil Service reformers and progressives alike embraced executive administration as a primary mechanism by which to secure improved efficiency and effectiveness in the dispatch of the public's business. The technical expertise and political neutrality required to achieve such goals, however, seemed to demand an important measure of insulation from the popular will. Such insulation conflicted with the imperative of democratization—movement away from a party-based patronage and spoils system and toward "the people." Mosher wrestled with this fundamental ambiguity—which, of course, is mirrored in the construction of the nation's constitutional framework—throughout his life. Tellingly, he did so most often through the analytic lens of history.

For Mosher, the study of history appeared to provide context, understood both in terms of how and why a specific organization had come to its present situation *and* how regime and societal currents had produced imperatives which shaped the capacities and sphere of action of those with responsibility to act. History, if it teaches nothing else, warns the analyst against an undue belief in the plasticity of his or her surroundings. Mosher seemed to assume that an organization or a decisionmaker, in effect, was dealt a hand by history and only within that context could it, he, or she expect to exercise discretion. The special challenge implicit in that reality lies in how the decisionmaker defines and approaches the situation and the conflicts occurring within it. If a context is accurately assessed, discretion can be exercised responsibly to maximal effect. History was not fully determinative. Neither, however, were officials radically free to pursue their individually determined ends.

Mosher also appeared to look to history as the only reliable provider of examples of action with potential utility to address current concerns. History was all the scholar had ready at hand that was meaningful and that could permit the forecasting of problems and the development of recommendations concerning them.

Mosher scoured history for what it might reveal about the essential nature of the enterprise of public administration in its dynamic context. He analyzed antecedents seeking to discover what mechanisms and patterns of thought were evidenced there. These he explored in detail, for their import for real people with decision-making responsibilities. Put another way, Mosher appears to have employed historically informed analysis in the service of those called upon to administer the democratic state. Events were not significant for themselves but instead for what each might reveal about the role of public servants or the context in which they worked.

Simultaneously, he examined the lessons of history as these were revealed in major currents of change within society. Those trends, in turn, placed certain identifiable stresses and constraints on the structuring and operation of institutions. For the analyst, to attempt to assay how patterns of thought and change affected and shaped institutions and the decisionmakers within them was tantamount to providing an opening statement to an ongoing dialogue on the most vital concerns confronting a democratic nation. That public dialogue was critical, for only through debate and discussion could the contours of change be understood and purposive action be undertaken. No one individual could gather all of the necessary information or possess sufficient imagination to address all of the relevant concerns by himself or herself....

Certain of Mosher's works are examined here with an eye to how each reflected three major areas of interest or themes to which he frequently returned throughout his career. These related closely to both the central reform dilemma and how he seems to have conceived of the field:

- public management techniques and needs and how these might best be served through research,
- the public service, education, and the public interest,
- the public service in the constitutional system.

Each of these themes is introduced briefly below. Each idea was selected because it consistently appeared throughout his published works. The three subjects are interrelated. Other conceptual streams also appear in Mosher's writings. However, this article focuses on these themes because they reflect significant ideas that Mosher frequently addressed over the course of his career. After introducing each major area of interest, the article examines several of Mosher's important publications (again, not all of his writings nor even all of his significant works are analyzed here) in light of these themes at different stages of his career. Throughout, Mosher's intellectual growth is accompanied by a broadening vision of the scope and character of public administration. His view of the field emerged over time and grew enormously in sophistication and complexity. By the close of his career—he was intellectually active until his death—Mosher had constructed a rich and compelling view of the role of the public service and public servants, within the context of the nation's constitutional framework. A final section of the article provides an initial set of observations concerning the legacy of Mosher as an intellectual, educator, and public servant.

THE MAJOR THEMES OF MOSHER'S WORKS

Public Management Research and Practice

Mosher was ever concerned with how the public service could serve the broader society. He sought consistently to blend a respect for the role of the public official with a deep awareness of the unique requirements implied by the special status of that position. For Mosher, public officials were professionals with special capabilities and, perhaps most importantly, special responsibilities, not shouldered by others whose role did not demand that they serve the polity as a whole. Therefore, research concerning the enterprise of public management had always to serve a broader imperative than simple utility—yes, it must be useful, it must "work"—but it had also to serve the special requirements of a uniquely accountable public service.

The Public Service, Education, and the Public Interest

For its part, the public service for Mosher represented not merely a job but an endeavor and a challenge worthy of the highest respect and societal esteem. Given that perspective, he was keenly interested in exploring the ever changing role of the public service both to understand its needs more fully and to chart more comprehensively its many contributions to the citizenry it serves.

He did not need, therefore, to venture far conceptually from his abiding interest in understanding the role of the public service to identify a need to assure that the most highly qualified professionals operated that service. Mosher consistently sought to draw linkages between the status of the nation's public service and the changing nature of education for that career path. He was always interested in attracting and preparing the best and the brightest for national (and state and local) public service and in assuring that such a career would be worthy of their respect. Education held the highest promise for equipping the nation's future decisionmakers with the knowledge necessary to tackle the mounting needs confronting the polity. Therefore, those interested in the field of public administration ought naturally to care deeply about *how* young men and women were educated for public life.

The issue was not, however, simply what to teach potential public servants. It went much deeper than that. As Mosher remarked in the preface to the second edition of *Democracy and the Public Service*, the recruitment and education of the public's workforce was critical to the adequate functioning of the nation:

> The problem of making government behave in the best interests of its members—that is, we the people—is the problem of democracy. A major part of that problem is the work and the decisions of those who perform as our agents—the public service (Mosher, 1982, pp. xi-xii).

It was not enough to recruit the most capable to the public service, for with the job came enormous responsibility. For the field of public administration, that obligation implied a need to educate future public servants broadly to an understanding of the special character of their role. Each public service professional was charged not simply to determine and reflect public opinion but to educate and lead that opinion where necessary and appropriate. The benchmark for all civic action was ultimately the public good—something greater than any single interest and more than the sum of the specific positions of professional or societal groups. As Bruce Hackett observed in his review of the first edition of *Democracy,* Mosher assumed that the professions could take care of themselves but the question remains as to who or what will care for the majority of the population still lacking the proper credentials. Continuing to nourish commitment to some conception of the public interest would seem, in this view, to be both a moral and political necessity (1970, p. 643).

The Public Service in the Constitutional System

Perhaps no matter more concerned Mosher during the final two decades of his life than describing the impact of the changing nature of American politics on the nation's central administrative institutions. Mosher's sustained interest in the U.S. General Accounting Office (GAO) and the U.S. Office of Management and Budget (OMB) arose precisely because the operation of these institutions—placed as they are at the center of the American political scene—allowed him to explore the tensions and challenges confronting the public service in a swiftly changing and intensely political context. These lead agencies serve the nation's executive, legislative, and judicial branches and exercised enormous responsibilities in governmental policymaking and administration. Their environment, like their aims and reach, was as large as the nation's political system.

PUBLIC MANAGEMENT RESEARCH AND PRACTICE

Mosher began his professional career as a practitioner, not an academician. Upon graduation from Dartmouth College in 1934, he obtained a post with the Tennessee Valley Authority. After returning to graduate school at Syracuse University to obtain his master's degree in 1938, Mosher served in the Army Air Force during the Second World War. Following that conflict, he worked for the United Nations Relief and Rehabilitation Administration, the Public Administration Clearinghouse, and the City of Los Angeles before returning to Harvard University to complete his Doctor of Public Administration degree. Only then, in 1950, after

15 years of public service, did Mosher launch his academic career. As he embarked upon a "second" career as a scholar, Mosher could draw upon a varied and very substantial reservoir of practical experience. That array of experience informed his scholarship from the start.

Mosher's scholarly approach to public management eschewed the narrow specializations of then contemporary practice in favor of an integration of personnel and staffing, planning, and resourcing. Like all MPA-trained professionals of his generation, he entered a public service in which few practitioners were trained at all and those who were trained were expected to move freely from one position or area to another. His own graduate training at Syracuse University provided a solid understanding of orthodox thinking with a heavy emphasis on the role of the executive in government and within organizations.

His early career as a practitioner was broadened conspicuously by his continuing interest in research and in the development of the field of public administration. These interests, in turn, arose partly from his acquaintance with leading figures in the discipline because of his father's position (William E. Mosher was the first Dean of the Maxwell School of Citizenship and Public Affairs of Syracuse University) and partly from his native curiosity.

Two of Mosher's early published works, *City Manager Government in Rochester, New York* (1940) and *Program Budgeting in Theory and Practice* (1954), reveal his abiding interest in examining both how administrative systems actually worked and in discerning broader lessons from such findings. Many observers now consider both efforts classics.

City Manager Government (Mosher's master thesis) examined the impact of adoption of a city manager plan on Rochester administration. Mosher argued that

> The City Manager plan was much more than a new form of government; it was the banner around which the forces for political reform could rally (1940, p. 92).

Paradoxically, many reformers were less than pragmatic in their expectations and, therefore, quite cynical about what had, in fact, been achieved by adoption of the plan. To understand the significance of the ideals pressed by the plan's proponents, Mosher contended, the reform group's initiatives had to be measured not against their too romantic aims but against specific improvements in the city's governance. While the utopia of nonpartisan government had not been achieved, Mosher reported a number of solid

> ... achievements in the administrative realm [including] the integration of financial functions under the administrative hierarchy and the strengthening of financial controls, notably the budget (1940, p. 94).

Rochester was the scene of an important experiment to improve management practice through major political change. Mosher evenhandedly evaluated the results of the initiative. What appears most to have engaged his attention as an analyst was the practical purport of change for the delivery of real services to the city's citizenry.

Mosher's analysis neatly demonstrated how reformers' broader-gauged concerns were directly relevant to the everyday successful exercise of authority by the city's responsible decisionmakers. Mosher was able to illuminate the broad consequences of change for the city's routine administration.

Mosher's important and influential *Program Budgeting in Theory and Practice* was published in 1954. The effort, a revision of his doctoral dissertation, drew upon extensive interviews with Defense Department budget officials and traced the import of substantial changes in the organization and processes of military decision making. In particular, Mosher sought to examine the significance of the new unified command structure for budgeting in the Department of the Army. He dispassionately evaluated the consequences of the new allocation system for the institutions that were charged with its use.

> The budget, in its rise to near-dominance, has picked up new functions and a greatly enlarged role. It may well be that the single budget process has been overloaded with

different kinds of problems not basically consistent with each other.... The two purposes of budgeting, the making of program decisions and the provision of an effective system of administration, must be linked, but they should not have to ride the same track at the same time. The present attempt to use the same vehicle for both kinds of purpose is detrimental to both (1954, pp. 236-237).

In this work, as in his *Rochester* effort, Mosher analyzed the implications of significant political and structural change for administrative decision making. He appeared to seek to understand thoroughly what was happening in each situation and then to offer pragmatic assessments of the implications of those findings for efficient and effective management. Mosher's concern to understand the context of management was undertaken with the realities and challenges of everyday administration firmly in view. Mosher next undertook this sort of analysis not with an eye to a specific agency or city but, instead, with a focus on the development of the field of public administration.

Mosher provided a now-classic analysis of the field's development early in his "academic" career in a 1956 *Public Administration Review* article entitled "Research in Public Administration: Some Notes and Suggestions." Employing a number of elements that would later characterize his work—a focus on the evolution of public administration as a field of study characterized by a common body of identifiable needs, challenges, and concerns, careful attention to, and marshalling of, historical evidence, and a broad understanding of related fields of study—Mosher offered a synopsis of the tradition of research in public administration and suggested a number of directions which those in the field might consider further.

Mosher contended that public administration as a field had reached a watershed in the early 1950s. Both changes in governmental policy and structure and intellectual developments had rendered the dominant (and rather limited) normative research tradition of the field inadequate. The orthodoxy bequeathed by the Bureau Movement and reformism had, in Mosher's view, run its course. A new analytical awareness and eclecticism of approach, based in part on the burgeoning social sciences, led Mosher to describe the state of administrative research this way: "The garden is extensive and sprawling with flowers of many kinds and hues. It more nearly resembles an old-fashioned dooryard than a well-tailored promenade" (1956, p. 177).

In less colorful prose, Mosher contended that research in public administration had crossed a threshold from which there could be no return. It was and would remain more diverse in perspective than before:

> Much study of the earlier sort—directed to efficiency, structure, orderliness, and localized problem-solving—continues, perhaps as much as ever. Many of the pragmatic types of projects today, however, lay greater emphasis upon economic, social, and behavioral factors. Increasing attention has been given to non-normative studies of administrative behavior, politics and administration, organization structure, and like subjects (1956, p. 171).

Mosher's 1956 assessment of the research needs of the field serves as a useful metaphor for his own intellectual development. In that essay he wondered: "Is there a 'field' of public administration, or, in the academician's glossary, is there such a 'discipline'? If so, what is its scope, its rubric, its method?"

In addressing this query, Mosher analyzed the paradox implicit in attempting to bound public administration:

> Any definition of the field would be either so encompassing as to call forth the wrath or ridicule of others, or so limiting as to stultify its own disciples. Perhaps it is best that it not be defined. It is more an area of interest than a discipline, more a focus than a separate science. Like administration itself, the study of administration must employ a variety of methods and approaches. It is necessarily cross-disciplinary (1956, p. 177).

Perhaps the same may be said of Mosher's intellectual role. As a writer, thinker, and researcher, he is extremely difficult to characterize in any facile way. His writings were wide ranging and often crossed traditional disciplinary lines. As often, his efforts were prompted, at least initially, by his recognition of a property of peculiar intellectual interest or significance in a serious practical problem at hand. His works and the range of his interest, like those of the field he sought to describe, were catholic. Just as Mosher could contend that public administration had matured to a point that its researchers could now confidently proclaim (and embrace) new forms of vitality in their many variants, so too can it be said that with publication of his article in *PAR*, Mosher began to traverse new intellectual terrain.

"Research in Public Administration" saw Mosher deepen and broaden many of the defining characteristics of reform-era public administration. He still viewed public administration as a professional field, less a science than an activity whose exact dimensions were determined by changes in policy and program. Research was valuable as a central vehicle by which to improve practice. Nevertheless, Mosher contended that public administration research had to embrace the methods of the social sciences and to define its needs broadly while recognizing many shared interests with other disciplines. Even though public administration's interest in research may indeed be more utilitarian than that of other disciplines, he saw a significant convergence of concerns "at the deeper level of value orientation and in the selection of research problems. The other social sciences in the past two decades have been increasingly concerned with social problems and action research, a focus not unlike that of administration" (1956, p. 174).

Mosher defined useful research broadly and that definition certainly included case studies. He supported the development of case material in his early teaching days at Syracuse University, primarily as a pedagogical device to supplement the thin contemporary literature available for graduate instruction in the field. By the late 1950s, interest in such studies had begun to focus on their potential for scientific research—that is to say, their utility in constructing and testing hypotheses and advancing generalizable findings about administration.

Max O. Stephenson, Jr. and Jeremy F. Plant

In 1958, the Executive Board of the Inter-University Case Program (ICP) approached Mosher to request that he lead an effort to assess the usefulness of the case method in advancing understanding of administrative behavior in complex public organizations. Working with a Research Committee composed of five outstanding scholars, he organized a volume containing 12 cases on reorganization. Mosher personally contributed an introduction concerning the case method, a case analysis and a longer "analytical commentary" on organizations.

The edited book that resulted from the project, *Governmental Reorganizations: Cases and Commentary*, appeared in 1967. The effort represented an opportunity to explore many of the research issues Mosher had initially treated in 1956. First, the case method was employed in as systematic a manner as possible, focusing on a typology of reorganizations accepted by all contributors to the project; a clear set of major terms defined as precisely as possible; and, for the first time in a collection of case studies, a hypothesis that would be treated by the cumulative weight of the evidence of analyses. Mosher labeled that guiding proposition "the participation hypothesis":

> Government reorganizations involving intended changes in individual behaviors and relationships are more effective, both structurally and substantively, when the persons whose behaviors are expected to change take part in the process of reaching decisions as to what the change will be and how it will be made (1967, p. xvii).

Three working assumptions underscored and clarified the main hypothesis: that participation in the reorganization process is most relevant to persons and groups directly affected by change; that participation is most effective if it leads to a close correspondence of individual group and organizational goals; and that participation should begin as early in the reorganization process as possible to be effective.

Governmental Reorganizations was, and remains, a fascinating book. The preface (by Edwin A. Bock) and Mosher's introduction outlined the history of the case method. The analyses themselves are among the best-researched and written examples of the genre. At least two of the chapters, in fact, have attained the status of classics: E. Drexel Godfrey's "The Transfer of the Children's Bureau" and Mosher's own "The Reorganization of the California State Personnel Board" (1967, pp. 149-165; 397-439).

The third section of the work contained Mosher's analytical commentary, the most complete discussion of organizations extant in his writings. Divided into three chapters on organizations, organizational change, and participation and reorganization, his perceptive commentary does far more than discuss the significance of participation as a factor in reorganization.

Mosher identified several caveats as lessons to be gleaned from the project. The first of these was that participation was not an independent variable that explained reorganization outcomes. Rather,

> its positive or negative effects in large organizations depend upon a great many other factors such as: the nature and purposes of the organization; the source of initiative for reorganization; and the intent of the reorganizers; the orientations of the people concerned; the content of the reorganization proposed; the stages of reorganization at which participation is, or is not, practiced; and others (1967, p. 471).

Mosher's second caveat concerned the enthusiasm with which the field of public administration was embracing theories of organization and behavior which ignored or downplayed the distinctively *public* character of government agencies. He was skeptical of an approach to organization that did not consider service to the broader community as a distinguishing characteristic. As he noted, "my approach and my emphasis lay stress upon differences from, rather than likenesses to, much current organization theory" (1967, p. 471).

This use of the case method to examine reorganization raised anew the issue of the distinctiveness of public organizations but did not resolve with any certitude how public administration might be distinguished from other sorts of administrative activity. As Mosher commented in his final paragraph:

> The cases suggest that there are basic differences between public and business organizations arising from: nature of purpose; degree and nature of political exposure; nature of legal, administrative, and political control; leadership personnel; and attitudes and motivations of employees. But such contracts are largely inferential and indirect (1967, p. 527).

THE PUBLIC SERVICE, EDUCATION, AND THE PUBLIC INTEREST

Mosher's research on decision making and organizational change in the 1960s caused him subtly, but increasingly and perceptibly, to abandon analysis of relatively narrow issues of management process and programming in favor of issues of systemwide importance: professionalism and the concept of the public service; the impact of administration on society and the maintenance of democratic values at a time of rapid change. Two seminal works of this period demonstrated the continuing maturation of his scholarship: *Democracy and the Public Service* (1968; revised in 1982) and "The Public Service in the Temporary Society" (1971).

Democracy and the Public Service combined Mosher's gift for historical research with his ability to define concepts rigorously and to create useful analytic categories. It is not necessary here to repeat his penetrating examination of professionalism in the development of the public service in the United States. What is important for present purposes about the analysis in *Democracy* are its conclusions about the emergence of the professional state and the underlying role of education within it.

> Each profession is learning the hard way of its own inadequacies and its underlying dependence upon the methods and understandings of other disciplines. The

interdisciplinary and interprofessional approach is no longer a mere academic curio, an interesting but dilettantish experiment. In today's world, it is an absolute necessity.... The interconnection of social problems and the interdependence of disciplines in dealing with them are two sides of the same coin (1968, pp. 126-217).

The multifaceted challenge confronting America's profession-based public service was then, and has remained, how it will reconcile its own in-bred specialism with the complex multidimensional problems for which it has been given an increasing measure of responsibility. The professions, indeed the professional public service, represented for Mosher an important intermediary between the state and the individuals who operated its institutions. One profound implication of that fact was obvious. To train or to educate professionals to specific roles was to define how a large share of the public's work would be accomplished. The nation's colleges and universities could recognize that fact and prepare their students accordingly, or the public service could be left bereft of any unifying vision. Mosher feared that simple inertia might allow the latter of these possibilities to occur. Higher education, or at least professional education, had slowly shifted toward excessive specialization and vocationalism and away from humanism and general culture. This trend had come at considerable cost.

In "The Temporary Society," Mosher refined the line of historical thought first presented in *Democracy* and provided an analysis of the recent past and present that put much of the ferment of public administration of the time in perspective. At a time when advocacy and attachment to one's perspective was *de riguer*, "The Temporary Society" was detached and analytical. In a masterpiece of understatement, Mosher stated his purpose as simply: "... to cull from our experience of the last few years—the decade of the '60s—some probabilities about the next few—the decade of the '70s; and to deduce from these what we (in public administration) should be doing about it" (1971, p. 47)....

"Temporary Society" represented a powerful call to look anew and broadly at the field of public administration during a time of profound change. In a paragraph that still rings true, Mosher summarized his view of this perceptive:

> To recapitulate: the emerging public administration, the truly "new" public administration, will bear responsibilities of a range and an importance that are hardly suggested in any current textbook. It will have to anticipate and to deal with changes in a society that is changing more rapidly than any in human history. It, too, will have to be rapidly changeable and flexible. It will have to press for greater rationality and develop and utilize even more sophisticated tools for rational decisions, at the same time accommodating to forces that seem unrational. It must concern itself more than in the past with human goals "life, liberty, and the pursuit of happiness"—but without damage to the processes which make democracy viable. And these goals must be more sophisticated than simple quantitative growth. It must recognize the functional and geographic interdependence of all sectors of the society without too much sacrifice to the values of professional specialism and local interest. It must develop collaborative workways whereby centralization and decentralization proceed simultaneously, and assure high competence at every level of government (1971, p. 52).

He concluded the essay by echoing a theme first introduced in *Democracy* concerning the implications for higher education of his analysis of the changing public service. He explicitly rejected a conception of the field as a branch of management. Mosher argued that a genuinely new approach to education for public service was unfolding in the various schools of public affairs which had begun to emerge in the 1960s:

> They will not be a resurrection of the earlier efforts to create a profession built around POSD-CORB, nor of current efforts to create a management science based either on sociological theory of organizations or on

operations research and PPBS—although all of these will play a part. They will be grounded rather in an understanding of social values, social and governmental institutions, and the mechanisms of induced social and political change; in a sensitivity to the feelings and desires of others, both as groups and individuals and the capacity to reason and work with them in finding and effectuating solutions to problems. They will be motivated by an unremitting search for that elusive but holy ghost, the public interest. They will rely upon the study of problems and the application to those problems of varieties of research techniques, methodologies, and disciplinary and professional perspectives. And this will involve working through and around the multifold obstacles and roadblocks of other human beings generally, and governmental institutions particularly (1971, pp. 61-62).

Here, in *Democracy*, and in a 1972 article, "'End Product' Objectives of Pre-Entry Professional Education for Urban Administration and their Implications for Curriculum Focus"—surely the least mellifluous title of any Mosher work—the underlying theme was always the same: the public service requires both specialized professionals to attack specific problems *and* generalist executives who combine expertise with a broader and deeper perspective on public affairs. Government was experiencing a "geometrically increasing growth in the need for people capable of visualizing longer and broader goals, of identifying the interconnections of different specialized activities, and of coordinating and integrating specialized activities toward those goals" (1972, pp. 151-152).

Mosher's interest in achieving a commonly accepted view of public administration as a field necessarily (and properly) concerned with democratic values, systems, and institutions, managed by broadly educated political-administrative generalists had by the late 1960s led him explicitly to apply historical analysis to the field, an effort first undertaken in earnest in *Democracy*. Three efforts of this sort engaged him between 1972 and 1976: the *New Federalist Papers* project; a book of essays on the development of the theory and practice of public administration—written for the 50th anniversary of the Maxwell School (edited by Mosher in 1975) under the title *American Public Administration: Past, Present, Future* (1975a)—and a panel at the 1976 ASPA National Conference that featured two classic and complementary studies that applied historical analysis to public administration. Lynton K. Caldwell contributed "Novus Ordo Seclorum: The Heritage of American Public Administration and American History: A Century of Professionalism" for Mosher's panel. Both essays later appeared in a special issue of *Public Administration Review* devoted to the nation's bicentennial (1976a). . . .

The introduction to *American Public Administration: Past, Present, Future* illustrated Mosher's growing interest in using history as a guide for the future across a canvas much more expansive than traditional public administration. The dominant theme of the volume was the continuing development of public administration as practice and profession, yet he contended vigorously that the field had soon to consider its limitations, to accept "the growing realization within each discipline and profession of its innate inability to handle real problems of the world within its own traditional confines. Those problems stubbornly refuse to respect academic, professional, and vocational boundaries" (1975a, p. 5). To capture adequately the context of which it was necessarily a part, public administration could ill afford to define itself in technical or formal terms. The need for a broader vision, which history was certain to inform, was urgent—and paramount—lest the field sink into irrelevance or worse.

Mosher had always considered the executive function an important point at which professional management intersected with political leadership. The essence of the executive role is to generalize from a variety of specialized perspectives and to provide purpose and direction to organizations. In these works, he exhibited a willingness to link administrative and political contexts. These contexts, in turn, both reflected and shaped still broader sociocultural currents. The role of executive leadership provided a useful lens through which such linkages might be examined.

The 1970s soon revealed a significant aspect of the executive function: the impact of executive action on ethics and values.

Along with the turbulence arising from the pace and dynamic of change, as described in "The Temporary Society," came the controversy emanating from the struggles of a political system to confront what Mosher (and many others) considered one of the most serious challenges to American popular government since the Civil War: the Watergate affair.

Mosher saw in the Watergate scandal a dangerous convergence of three major factors: the suspicion and antagonism toward governmental activities that is deeply embedded in American political culture; the growing demand, nevertheless, that government address important social issues; and, in the bungled break-in itself, evidence of a tendency within the White House to lose sight too often of the fundamental rights of the many in favor of providing special benefits to a few—whether legally or not.

Working with Congress through the National Academy of Public Administration in response to an invitation by Senator Sam Ervin, chair of the Senate Subcommittee on Presidential Campaign Activities, Mosher chaired a blue-ribbon panel whose deliberations resulted in a thorough report concerning the Watergate crisis. That volume, shepherded and authored by Mosher, supported an abbreviated and circumscribed Executive Office of the President that would have consisted of a small number of staff advisers, working alongside department and agency heads with clearly defined line duties. In wording which echoed the first offered in 1937 by the President's Committee on Administrative Management, Mosher suggested that "the functions of the Executive Office of the President should be to assist the President, not to be the general manager of the executive branch" (1974, p. 41). Mosher sought to avoid the commingling of political campaign organizations and judicial offices with the political executive by establishing new formal arrangements to keep the Justice Department and campaign organizations at arms length from the President.

Aside from these specific recommendations, the Watergate report was significant in Mosher's career because of the breadth of its focus. The effort found him writing and thinking about the entire workings of the American system of governance including, among other topics, the role and functioning of its political parties, the changing nature of the presidency, interbranch relationships, and campaigns and elections. Interestingly, however, Mosher saw the role of the public service and an accompanying ethic of civic virtue as essential to an adequate national response to the challenges posed by Watergate. As he remarked:

> One cannot legislate ethical behavior, although laws may and do set outer boundaries of permissible behavior and provide incentives for compliance—as well as penalties for violation.... Some of the options considered in this report involve statutory change; a few, constitutional amendment. But many are exhortations that those in public office or seeking public office may behave responsibly and with devotion and integrity (1974, p. 15).

Similarly, Mosher closed the volume by quoting approvingly Thomas Jefferson's well-known commentary on ethics: "Whenever you are to do a thing, though it can never be known but to yourself, ask yourself how you would act were all the world looking at you and act accordingly" (1974, p. 126).

Watergate brought into view for Mosher a range of concerns that, while in an important sense organizational—even constitutional—nevertheless also properly fell within the purview of individual responsibility. The crisis could be analyzed in political, institutional, and administrative terms, but ultimately important recourse lay with the officials—individuals—who operated within that complex context. Nevertheless, one could not understand adequately the actions of those individuals without also addressing the larger group of participants and organizations of which they were but a part. It was this larger universe that he now explored and in which he saw the civil servant operating. Both vantage points were necessary—that of the individual and that of the context in which he or she operated—in order to understand events as they actually unfolded. If his vision had become broader, Mosher's work also exhibited a fresh imperative to view government and administration from the perspective of the individuals whose efforts animated it. Institutions are critical, but they are given life by officials whose attitudes they reflect. If attitudes are changed, institutional change will follow, even if fitfully. This important theme of Mosher's Watergate analysis would again figure prominently in his last three major works undertaken during the 1980s.

Not coincidentally, perhaps, the dynamic tension or dialectic implicit in the relationship of civil official and institution or between elected official and constitutional framework mirrored Mosher's bedrock concern to address somehow the central dilemma of public administration: viz., how can the democratic imperative be reconciled with the requirements of leadership and professional expertise? The similar dialectical tensions between the scope for individual responsibility and action and structural constraints and between expertise and democratic responsiveness in turn appeared to reflect Mosher's view of the possibilities imposed by the workings of history. Each of these tensions, images of one another, fascinated Mosher throughout his career. Each recurs throughout his writings.

THE PUBLIC SERVICE IN THE CONSTITUTIONAL SYSTEM

The second half of the 1970s and the 1980-1990 period—the final decade of his life—saw Mosher produce a remarkable outpouring of scholarship. The nation's Bicentennial year witnessed publication of the first of two edited volumes concerning the development of the field to 1950, *Basic Documents of Public Administration: 1776-1950* (1976b). The final year of the decade saw publication of his definitive portrait of the role and evolution of a leading staff agency, *The GAO: The Quest for Accountability in American Government* (1979).

During the first year of the new decade, Mosher produced one of the most important articles to appear in the field in many years. "The Changing Responsibilities and Tactics of the Federal Government" was a provocative and far-ranging analysis that has been widely cited and will undoubtedly remain influential for years to come (1980). "Changing Responsibilities" was followed the next year by the second volume in his documentation of the evolving character of the field, *Basic Literature of Public Administration:*

1787–1950 (1981). In 1982, the second edition of *Democracy and the Public Service* was published. *A Tale of Two Agencies: The General Accounting Office and the Office of Management and Budget* (1984) was Mosher's next major work. That effort, a carefully documented comparative analysis of the genesis and maturation of the U.S. General Accounting Office (GAO) and the U.S. Bureau of the Budget–U.S. Office of Management and Budget (BOB-OMB), was completed in 1984. Mosher's last major book, *Presidential Transitions and Foreign Affairs*, appeared in 1987 and was co-authored with W. David Clinton III and Daniel G. Lang. That work, characteristically wide-ranging and discerning, demonstrated the continuing vitality of his intellect and his outstanding capacity to integrate ideas across commonly accepted boundaries and across time.

Taken together, Mosher's final 15 years of scholarship outstrip in energy, originality, and insight even the remarkable first 15 years of his career during which he restlessly explored his talents and intellectual interests. The 1980s, especially, saw him revisit and deepen his reflections on by-now-familiar themes. It is useful to divide the pieces under discussion into rough groupings consisting of three sets of twins and one additional work.

The first set of twins was comprised of the two volumes concerning the growth of the field. Mosher saw these texts as a means by which to introduce a larger audience to the documents and literature that had stood the test of time. Curiously, to that date, no edited collection of the sort he undertook existed. As he observed in the preface to the *Basic Documents* volume:

> With the recent proliferation of texts and edited collections of readings in or related to public affairs and administration, one may reasonably question: why now this one? The rationale is that there is a serious lacuna in the spate or recent literature in its failure to treat seriously and systematically the older documents, official and unofficial, which have proven to have lasting impact upon knowledge and understanding in this field (1976b, p. vii).

Mosher did not intend that the *Basic Documents* book or its companion, *Basic Literature*, constitute a history of the field. Instead, their purpose was "to provide the most relevant materials for scholars and students interested in the development of the field, materials that are hard or in some places impossible to come by and are nowhere collected" (1986b, p. vii).

Collecting and editing these efforts gave Mosher cause to organize and to consider afresh his thinking concerning the historical development of the discipline. They offered an opportunity to reflect once again upon the intellectual roots of public administration. That chance for contemplation proved propitious, for it provided a helpful backdrop for Mosher's second set of twin analyses—this time of the GAO and OMB. These agencies were progeny of the same landmark statute, The Budget and Accounting Act of 1921.

Mosher completed the General Accounting Office volume first. The book traced the history of the GAO. However, Mosher's ambitions for the effort were higher than simply to provide a well-crafted chronicle of an important institution. He revealed his hope in the subtitle of the work: *The Quest for Accountability in American Government*. In fact, the book was really two books, for it consisted of "two interdependent parts: a history, and an analysis of the current situation" (1979, p. xvii). And it was the second part which most intrigued its author:

> Particularly in recent years, the potential sweep of GAO's concerns has become almost as broad as that of the federal government itself. I have found this study particularly revealing of how our system of government works, what it does, and the problems attending its decisions and actions. . . . I very much hope that this document will contribute as much to the understanding of American government as it does to the understanding of GAO (1979, p. xvii).

The GAO as central institution became for Mosher both metaphor and symbol for many of the challenges and changes confronting the public service and the constitutional system. He consciously undertook to examine thoroughly a leading agency with a special role in insuring accountability in order to reach larger—and enduring—questions besetting the nation.

While he could not discern how GAO would serve the citizenry in the future, Mosher was willing to identify "some of the factors, largely growing out of history, that are relevant to those who will have a hand in shaping its future" (1979, p,. 261). These factors included the agency's growing interdependence with its environment, including its rising reliance on other levels of government and other organizations to achieve its aims. Another crucial factor that had shaped the evolution of GAO and would do so in the future was the reality of the separation of powers. The very fact that Congress and the President represented discrete branches of government provided the office a reason to be, as well as scope for pressing its mandate. Many of the internal stresses and strains the agency had experienced over its history could be laid to its peculiar constitutional status and the growing reach of the role that it was required to serve.

Mosher's analysis of the roles and interdependencies of GAO with its environment may be equated with his larger concern with the linkages between the professional state and the broader society. As the Accounting Office's role broadened and deepened over the years, its workforce became far more professionally specialized. To understand the roles of GAO as an institution in its complex environment, the observer had first to understand the almost tautological relationship between the multifarious demands placed on the agency and the professional fractionation of its staff. That workforce, in turn, was dependent upon the institutions of higher education to prepare professionals for its ranks. As the jurisdiction and operating latitude of the agency grew, that nexus also grew in significance. The relationship of GAO to its environment, and of its personnel to the needs of society and to higher education symbolized for Mosher the vast network of interdependence which confronted those who would undertake to govern a heterogeneous nation.

A Tale of Two Agencies grew directly out of Mosher's experience with the GAO study. He had long held an interest in budgeting as a central vehicle by which a democratic society reveals its priorities and concerns and was intrigued by the fact that GAO and BOB-OMB, lead legislative and executive agencies, respectively, had been created at the same time and by the same act of Congress. This book sought explicitly to do for BOB-OMB what he had accomplished for GAO and then to compare the roles of these twins in their respective constellations and in the broader governmental system. Mosher outlined the reasons why he hoped that the work would prove of interest, in its introduction:

> The study of the two [agencies] together provides insights about the modern evolution of both the presidency and the Congress and also about the complexities of the relations between the two. Students of organization will be interested in the ways in which the two agencies have responded to external influences, in the stresses and strains of their internal structures and cultures, and particularly in their contrasting modes of, and problems in, bringing about basic internal changes (1984, p. ix).

These comments neatly captured the maturity of Mosher's scholarship. He was at once interested in GAO and BOB-OMB as institutions and organizations and as vehicles by which to gain insights into the evolution of the presidency and Congress. He sought not only to understand these agencies as singular entities but to analyze how each influenced and was structured by its interdependence with its political and societal context.

In *A Tale of Two Agencies*, perhaps to a degree unsurpassed elsewhere in his writings, Mosher sought systematically to capture internal agency culture and to relate that to broader professional and societal currents. The tension between the imperatives of democracy and the requirements of leadership and expertise provided the central theme of the book:

> A principal problem of both these agencies ... is the maintenance of continuity, expertise, and credibility on the one hand and of political responsiveness on the other: in short, the relating within the same organization of professionalism and politics without damage to either.

Such coexistence must be a common problem in those public agencies that require much knowledge and skill and whose costs and outputs are of public concern and controversial. Indeed, it must be a pervasive problem of government in all the developed and developing countries of the world (1984, p. ix).

The complex roles of these twin agencies, beholden to the executive and legislature, gave Mosher the opportunity to address the central ambiguity of the field of public administration at the point in the system of governance where it could most readily and deeply be examined. To analyze GAO and OMB was to study institutions

- whose internal structural complexities, strains, and tradeoffs were broadly representative of many other public agencies;
- whose roles prompted careful analysis of the changing character of other actors in the constitutional system;
- whose staffs could be considered reflections of the strengths and weaknesses of past development and possible future direction of the professional civil service.

One could, Mosher appeared to suggest, if one looked carefully and thoroughly enough, understand in the activities of these institutions the entire governmental system at work and within it, the special role being played by the professionalizing public service.

An important theme common to both of these works was Mosher's sensitivity to the role which changing individual attitudes and perspectives in concert with evolving societal trends play in institutional change. In *A Tale of Two Agencies* particularly, Mosher poked gentle fun at GAO and BOB-OMB alumni who, irrespective of when they worked there, all believed that their tenure represented the agency's "golden years." And, probably, Mosher wryly observed, each could be considered correct.

It seems to be a common foible to look back at certain periods of our lives with particular sentiment and cheer as the days of keen happiness and association. Thus, do many of us consecrate our childhood, our adolescence, our college days, our first days of marriage or parenthood, or even our lives that began at forty. (Notwithstanding that those days may have been filled with gloom and despair). The same is true of organizations and our association with them. We tend, I think, to glorify organizations when we were associated with them at their beginning or their reincarnations or when our own work was most important in them, and we have a tendency to believe that the organizations have been going downhill ever since (1964, p. 192).

Each successive generation of an agency's public servants understands its role differently from its predecessor and behaves differently in its changed societal and political context than does any of its antecedents. It matters little whether an objective observer might not concur in an alumnus' personal assessment of his or her institution's role at a specific point in time. What matters instead is *which* standard employees embrace to understand and to explain their own and their agency's activities. Modifications in that benchmark, in turn, bespeak significant change and serve as a map by which to understand the import of broader societal trends for institutional structure and behavior.

But the analyst cannot be content simply to trace shifts in individual attitudes. He or she must also seek to understand how individual beliefs and behaviors have interacted with changes in society to promote institutional innovation. A tension necessarily exists between the sweep of historical currents and the organization of resources on the public's behalf.

The last set of twins to be considered here includes Mosher's 1980 article, "The Changing Responsibilities and Tactics of The Federal Government" and the second edition of *Democracy and the Public Service* (1982). These are considered together because Mosher chose to cast the second edition of *Democracy* in terms of the major changes which had occurred in what the government was now doing and *how* it was doing it, which he had earlier outlined in "Changing Responsibilities." In that article, Mosher argued that the national government was fast "becoming a great and enveloping super-conglomerate with growing influence on the economy and society" (1980, p. 546). The fact, however, that much of what government now undertook it did through intermediaries; that it was "itself doing less but influencing far more" had enormous implications for both the coordination of public activities and the accountability of public action (1980, p. 547).

These changes augured a far more complex environment for public servants. The portent of the change in scope and character of public action was simply enormous. Indeed, Mosher seemed to contend, government and society were increasingly one and inseparable rather than distinct and independent:

> I would emphasize the growing interdependence of government with their clients and controllers, the American people. It is hard any more to distinguish what is private from what is public; what is national from what is international; what is federal from what is state or local; what is executive from what is legislative and what is judicial. I think it is not, as President Reagan suggests, a question of "getting government off our backs"; or as some public officials might say, if they dared, a question of "getting the people off our backs." We are meshed, interdependent, mutually intrusive. "We have found the government and it is us" (1982, p. xi).

The prospect of such interdependence and of such complexity did not, however, constitute cause for dismay or languor. The difficulties created by the new environment were

> ... challenging, not impossible nor even discouraging, and I devoutly hope that the focus in this book upon problems may not add to the dislike and disparagement of government and those who work for it which now seem so virulent among the United States population (1982, p. xii).

Mosher entered the second half of the 1980s concerned that the field of public administration self consciously reorient itself to the new management realities that confront it. A revolution had occurred, and all who cared about the character of the public service had to reorient their thinking accordingly. Their perspective, like the activities of the governments they wished to examine, must be deep and wide. The requirements of political responsiveness and the sheer dimensions of change required, as they had in 1956, new thinking about fundamental concerns: "It seems to me doubtful that many of us in public administration have kept sufficiently abreast of the problems and implications of the massive changes in American government—in our research, our literature, our teaching" (1980, p. 547).

Nothing less than a fresh vision for the field of public administration was now necessary. Novel forms and areas of research must be undertaken to explore a rapidly transforming entity. The information thus gathered should be used to inform those who exercised crucial responsibilities of the character of the enterprise in which they served:

> Most important of all is that our top public executives bring to their work an understanding of the public sector and the private, and of one level of government with others, both above and below. . . . Certainly there is a degree of interinvolvement—mutual intrusion if you prefer—of institutions seldom before experienced in American history. And public administrators at every level should be aware of it (1980, p. 547).

These comments underscore Mosher's continuing interest in the development of the field as well as his abiding belief that reason and education could continue to fulfill its needs.

Mosher's final major book saw him consider a number of familiar themes. *Presidential Transitions and Foreign Affairs* (1987) explicitly concerned the issue of how newly elected leaders and their appointees managed their relations with the careerist public service during periods of great consequence for the nation. Mosher and his colleagues examined every presidential transition from World War

Max O. Stephenson, Jr. and Jeremy F. Plant

Two through 1980 in an effort to plumb their significant commonalities as well as their implications for the United States in foreign affairs.

Significantly, this was not the first time that Mosher had concerned himself with the question of presidential transitions. In 1956 in his essay concerning the status of the field, "Research in Public Administration," Mosher had lamented the fact that so little analytic attention had been paid to the issue of transitions.

> Lulled by two decades of one-party continuity, many American students had seemingly forgotten that one of the purposes of the political system is to provide for turnovers of party leadership and transitions in administration. Concerned as some were to show that public administration is different from other kinds of administration, they had overlooked one overwhelming, yet elemental fact of difference—the orderly, calendared change in leadership as a result of election. Thought and technique had been developed for handling budgets, personnel, planning, and organization structure, but only the most incidental attention had been given to the phenomenon of political change. There had been little exploration of the problem of how the program of a newly elected party is translated into governmental policy and that into administration action (1956, pp. 171-172).

Three decades later, Mosher set out to address an important dimension of his earlier concern.

Once again, as in so many other of Mosher's works, a central analytic preoccupation was how best to reconcile the democratic impulse and imperative with that of professionalism and expertise. In this analysis, specifically, that issue translated into how best to balance a newly elected chief executives' impatient concern to press his foreign policy agenda with the reservoir of experience and knowledge contained in the nation's foreign service establishment. Too often, the equivalent of the nation's institutional memory has been dismissed as useless when presidential transitions occur. As Mosher and his coauthors asserted:

> It can also be observed that the career people in the foreign affairs agencies, particularly in the Foreign Service, are and long have been the central butt of the criticisms of the incoming presidential teams. They are seen as the groups least to be trusted. This situation is ironic because the success of every incoming team depends on them (1987, p. 252).

One of the central conclusions of this study echoed a major finding of Mosher's investigation of the Watergate tragedy. Indeed, the final chapter of *Presidential Transitions*, like that of the Watergate analysis a decade before, may be considered a call for a renewal of public spiritedness. Mosher exhorted elected officials and careerists alike to quicken or to renew their commitment to advancement of the public good through reasoned communication. The gulf between newly elected officials and career civil servants *could* be bridged, he argued, if both groups sought actively to do so with patience, tolerance, and forbearance. The tension between democracy and professionalism could be addressed effectively if all of the parties to the relationship sought to do so with openness and candor:

> One crucial element in the success of any transition is most often the spirit, the experience, and the wisdom of the newcomers. They must dispel their illusions that everything they find is bad and must be corrected; that their predecessors (and the career staff) are incompetent; that change in government can be easy and quick; and that government agencies should be run as nearly as possible like closed corporations, protected from congressional and public scrutiny (1987, p. 257).

What was crucial for all parties to understand, according to Mosher, was how critical their attitudes were to policy outcomes. With a positive outlook and enthusiasm for the public's business can come more open communication and an improved possibility for informed policy development and change.

Max O. Stephenson, Jr. and Jeremy F. Plant

But, just as with Watergate, the participants in transitions could not escape personal responsibility for the outcome of their joint efforts (or lack thereof). Transition organizations *are* important but no more so than those who design them. Those involved in changing administrations must come to understand that their experience is neither wholly unique nor utterly commonplace. Instead, each transition "is neither a complete halt nor a wholly new start, but only an interval in an ongoing history. Individuals and the particular administrations they serve are but transient elements in this continuing national development" (1987, p. 257).

The relationship between the new vanguard and the enduring institutions it must now lead is both extremely significant and equally evanescent. The character of the relationship between political responsiveness and professional expertise is inherently disputatious. But if both sets of participants are sufficiently sophisticated and open, many difficulties can be softened or overcome. Moreover, only recourse to a standard broader than their own specific interests is likely to allow participants to understand and to address their differences effectively. Mosher and his coauthors concluded: "These deficiencies can surely be ameliorated, but only if it is recognized that transitions form both an opportunity and a responsibility to serve the nation" (1987, p. 257).

In *Presidential Transitions*, Mosher employed history as a guide to the future. And, as in other major works, he appeared ultimately to place his confidence in the inculcation and refinement of a shared sense of duty among those—whether elected or appointed, careerist or not—who served the nation. In an important sense, that unselfishly motivated spirit of civic responsibility represented his fail-safe intellectual position, for one could always seek to educate professionals to respect it and to employ it as their common standard.

Mosher introduced *Presidential Transitions* by declaring that "the underlying quest of this study is for the optimum balance between change and continuity in the government of the American people" (1987, p. 2). Perhaps no single statement captures more eloquently Mosher's own analytic purpose during the last decade of his life.

CONCLUSION

What is the legacy of Frederick Camp Mosher? What ideas and insights will cause him to be remembered in the years to come? These few observations are organized around his contributions as intellectual, educator, and public servant.

Mosher as Intellectual

Mosher's major works were characterized by an unswerving determination to meet head-on the analytic challenges for public administration created by ceaseless political and societal change. Indeed, change itself must be considered an important construct in Mosher's writings. Much of what he explored, and often his rationale for examining it, was linked to the charting of rapid change. Since so much was in flux, the prudent scholar had to look to history to anchor his perceptions securely. History became the scalpel by which otherwise impenetrably interdependent and complex phenomena could be separated and examined and thereby rendered sensible and understandable.

Just as history could inform practice, it could apprise the analyst of the past experience and likely future directions of the field. Mosher returned again and again in his career to efforts which required that he think anew about where the discipline then stood and where it might be poised to go next. Whether consciously or not, Mosher's interest in the continuing development of the field as a totality kept him abreast of its cutting edge. And more often than not, that vantage point allowed him to contribute importantly to its literature and thinking.

Mosher's long-lived concern to address the ambivalent principles on which the field was founded proved to be the source of some of his most original scholarship. Mosher chose the concept of public professionalism to serve as intermediary between the antinomies of societal change and the demands of political responsiveness on the one hand and the fractionation and specialization required to address those needs on the other hand. Mosher applied the idea of professionalism to public administration with a rigor and breadth of imagination that made it a central concept of the field.

Mosher's notion of public professionalism also provided the conceptual grounding for an expansive definition of public administration. Professionalism was a means by which to link the technical side of management with concerns for ethical behavior and political responsiveness. It helped one to understand how the various elements of the American administrative state were inevitably linked to the nation's major political institutions and how the public service was integral to their effective functioning. Professionalism's demand for self-awareness and intellectual honesty required that public leaders see beyond short-term advantage, or clever manipulation of affairs of the moment, by becoming more conscious of connections to the past and their implications for the future. While he was unable to resolve the tensions at the core of the field of public administration, Mosher's sustained analysis of their ramifications shed important light on the functioning of the entire constitutional system and the role of administration within it.

Mosher as Educator

Mosher's response to the requirements of change was first to document it and then to educate a workforce with capacity to confront it effectively. He shared the Progressive vision of a world that could be affected by human action—and for the better. Whether declaring that a virtual revolution in how the government conducted its business had occurred or debating whether politicization had diminished OMB's role, Mosher consistently recurred to the power of the educational process to acquaint those who would serve with the vagaries of their role as well as to shape their attitudes and perspectives toward a vision much broader than that encompassed by any single individual or group interest.

Mosher as Public Servant

In an important sense, many who teach or write or work in public administration do so out of a desire to serve the citizenry at large. But in a relatively small field such as public administration, an individual's legacy may rest on far more than his or her published works. Frederick Mosher was, to the end, an accessible man who put great stock in working with others in the field. His work always benefited from his ability to listen, to maintain the closest and most constructive ties with other scholars and leading public servants. Detached in its analytic rigor, typically pragmatic referent, and historical awareness, Mosher's scholarship was never based on the often overblown claims of passing fashions or the need to debunk others.

Mosher remained to the end a faithful son of the civic spirit that spawned public administration. He based his studies on the compelling weight of carefully derived evidence: the changing nature of federal operations, trends in personnel recruitment and compensation, new approaches to staffing the Executive Office of the President, or the declining purchasing power of public executives. Yet, to all who knew him, it was clear that his scholarship was based upon a deeply rooted faith in the public service. Forced to endure in his last decade of life an ebb tide of public confidence and political support for public service, this faith kept him a productive, thoughtful, forceful, yet civil voice of reason.

Mosher expressed this faith in remarks presented at the annual conference of ASPA on 14 April 1986. Pointing to the erosion of support for public administration and the declining financial rewards of public employment, he still saw a profession based on an ideal of service to society.

> Finally, I would emphasize one big advantage of public service over most employment in the private sector. It is what George Frederickson and David Hart in a recent article in *PAR* referred to as the patriotism of benevolence. I prefer a little less ambitious title—simply service as in public service. When one works for government, his or her efforts are exerted not alone for self and family, but for others in the community, in the society. This kind of idealism has been a prime motivator in the development of this field from its self-conscious beginning in the early days of Luther Gulick and his colleagues. I grew up with it in my own home. In light

of the growing disparity of other rewards and of the brickbats thrown in the direction of the public service, it must still be a strong motivator. We can be grateful that so many able people are still entering public service and so many are staying there (1986, p. 4).

In that same spirit, Mosher dedicated *A Tale of Two Agencies* to

those men and women who through their careers in public service contribute beyond measure to the safety and welfare of the people of America and the world (1984).

That honest and simple gesture of recognition and respect revealed how deeply felt was Mosher's drive to assist and to support those who truly sought to serve. If such be an appropriate standard by which careers in this field may be judged, Mosher must surely be counted a member of that small group which represents its highest expression.

CHAPTER FIVE

The Changing Responsibilities and Tactics of the Federal Government[*]

FREDERICK C. MOSHER

INTRODUCTION

In decades gone by, most of what the federal government was responsible for and extended money for it did by itself through its own personnel and facilities. Consequently, much of the doctrine and the lore of federal management, like that of private enterprise, was based on the premise that its efficiency rested on the effective supervision and direction of its own operations. This was predominantly, though not exclusively, the case; federal administration has always worked with and operated through other governmental and nongovernmental institutions to some extent. The thesis of this article is that the changes since the beginnings of the New Deal and since World War II have been of such magnitude as to alter fundamentally the nature of federal responsibilities and modes of operating, calling for a quite different approach to the role of

---

Reprinted with permission from Public Administration Review *(November/December 1980, vol. 40, no. 6) © by the American Society for Public Administration (ASPA), 1120 G Street NW, Suite 700, Washington, DC 20005. All rights reserved.*

federal management in American society. The emphasis here is not upon freshly recognized (though old) social and economic problems and new public programs to respond to them—such as equal opportunity, health care, inflation, environment, energy, and others. It is upon the exploding responsibilities of the national government in virtually all functional fields and its carrying out of those responsibilities through, and interdependently with, nonfederal institutions and individuals.

I. FEDERAL SPENDING AND EMPLOYMENT[1]

Some of these changes are dramatically illustrated in the changing nature of federal expenditures.

The increases in federal outlays since the early post-World War II years have, on the surface, been enormous. Between 1949 and 1979, they grew by 13 times from $39 billion to $494 billion. The largest part of that growth was occasioned by inflation; in dollars of constant (1972) value, the outlays increased by almost three times from $106 billion to $280 billion. When related to the growth in the national economy, the growth in total budget outlays was considerably lower—from about 15 percent of the gross national product (GNP) to about 20 percent, or a total percentage increase of one-third. However, for the last 20 years the ratio of total federal outlays to GNP in constant dollars has been quite stable, hovering a little above or below 20 percent. Since the close of the Vietnam War, the ratio of total federal outlays to the gross national product has been quite stable, hovering a little above 20 percent.[2]

The growth of federal expenditures is, however, misleading. A substantial and increasing portion of them are not included in computing the GNP, even though the parts that are excluded have enormous indirect effects on the total economy. The only parts of federal budgetary expenditures that are counted in the GNP are payments for goods and services—that is, for the personal services of federal employees and for goods and other services purchased for federal use. The proportion of such federal payments to the GNP rose rapidly from about 8 percent in 1949, the last pre-Korean year, to almost 16 percent in 1953. Since that time, and except for a

Frederick C. Mosher

slight bump upward during the Vietnam struggle, the ratio has *persistently and greatly declined* to about 7 percent in 1979, lower than in 1949. The largest parts of both the rise and the decline have been payments for defense purposes, which, in 1979, comprised about two-thirds of all federal payments for goods and services. Such payments for purposes other than defense amounted to 2.4 percent of GNP in 1979, which compares with 2.8 percent in 1949.[3]

One further clue to what has been happening in the federal government lies in its employment statistics. Except for rather sharp increases followed by more moderate declines in connection with both the Korean and Vietnam wars, total civilian employment by the federal government has been remarkably stable for nearly three decades. Overall, it has grown slightly, but its growth has been at a lower rate than that of the American labor force and slightly lower than the growth of the total population that federal workers are presumed to serve. Measured in terms of numbers of federal civilian employees in the executive branch (including the Postal Service) per 1,000 in population, the figure for the end of 1979, 12.8, was the lowest since 1950, and the ratio is still very slightly declining.[4] The number of military personnel has of course dropped sharply since Vietnam and the institution of the all-volunteer armed forces. In relation to the total population, all civilian and military employment combined grew from 25 per 1,000 population in 1947 to 31 in 1957, to 32 in 1967. Since then it has dropped to 22 in 1979, a little below the ratio of 1947.[5]

These seemingly contradictory data—the increase in federal expenditures, the astonishing drop in the proportion of direct federal purchases to gross national product, and the gradually declining ratio of federal employment to population—are a consequence of fundamental shifts in the purposes, emphases, and methods of federal operations. In addition to its older, traditional functions, the federal government has become an enormous pump of money, which it receives mainly in the form of taxes (including insurance contributions) and borrowing, and pays to individuals and institutions, mostly in cash or loans according to a vast array of criteria that are different from each other and from those on which revenues are based. The fastest growing and currently the largest single portion of federal expenditures is labeled by economists as "transfer payments," not generally for services rendered the government but for the sustenance and benefit of the recipients and for reimbursements to those recipients of earlier contributions. In the quarter century of 1954 to 1979, these rose from 21 to 41 percent of federal expenditures; that is, from one- to two-fifths of the federal budget. The bulk of these are payments to individuals for social security, medicare, unemployment benefits, veterans' benefits, retirement, and a variety of other income support programs. Another kind of federal cash payments are those made for interest on the debt, basically payments for the use of borrowed money. Interest payments have risen slightly in relation to the total of federal spending and now amount to about 8 percent. But, when these two kinds of payments are combined, they account for about half of all federal expenditures.[6]

Another variety of federal payments consists of grants-in-aid to state and local governments. During the quarter century of 1952 to 1977, these grew in geometric proportions. In terms of current dollars, they nearly doubled every five years, rising from $2.9 billion in 1954 to $83 billion in 1979. In relation to total federal expenditures, they grew from 4 percent in 1954 to 17 percent in 1979. A very substantial proportion of the grants are, in effect, indirect transfer payments from the national government through state/local governments, to individuals for programs in housing, Medicaid, public assistance, nutrition, and others. Such indirect transfers are now rising from a little more than one-third (in 1979) to more than two-fifths (in 1982) of total grants-in-aid, and other grant programs are in fact declining in terms of constant dollars.

The only segment of federal expenditures that has significantly declined is purchases of goods and services, and here the shift has been dramatic. As a proportion of total expenditures, such payments dropped by more than half—from 73 percent in 1954 to 33 percent in 1979.

But this is only part of the story. A very substantial portion of purchases of goods and services consists of contracts and grants to institutions and individuals outside the federal government: to private businesses, universities, other nonprofit organizations, consultants, international organizations, foreign governments, and others. They are used for research and development, procurement of major equipment, construction of various kinds of public works, assistance to developing nations, payments to international organizations, and a multitude of other purposes.

It is not possible from current accounting practices and reports to make more than a very rough estimate of the costs of operations carried out by the government itself against those programs financed by the government but carried out wholly or largely by others. The best available information suggests that the two categories are not far from equal.[7] Of the net obligations incurred in 1979 ($584 billion), 14 percent ($81 billion) were for direct personal services and benefits (not including pensions for former personnel). Most or all of this could presumably be categorized as direct federal operations. On the other hand, the category of "Other" (contractual) Services" amounted to 16 percent ($85 billion) of total federal obligations for that year. Obligations for equipment, the bulk of which are produced outside the government, amounted to $31 billion, or 6 percent of total obligations.

According to a recent article in the *Washington Post* (24 February 1980, p. G1), the Federal Procurement Data System reported that the government spent "at least $74 billion on contracting in fiscal 1979, but officials say they expect the true figure is closer to $100 billion." If the former figure is correct, it would mean that nearly half of federal expenditures for goods and services is contracted out; if the latter is more nearly correct, about 60 percent of such expenditures is contracted out.

Some agencies, like the National Aeronautics and Space Administration and the Department of Energy (and its predecessors), have habitually relied upon private contractors for a large share of their activities. Most major federal construction, such as buildings and dams, is produced on contract. Most major equipment of the armed forces, including weapons systems, is produced by private contractors. Almost three-quarters of federal obligations for research and development, which totaled $23.5 billion in 1977, were allocated to industrial firms, universities, and other nonprofit institutions. Only 26 percent were conducted by the federal government itself in its own offices and laboratories.[8]

In summary, about half of all federal spending consists of payments for income security, interest on the debt, and similar direct transfers of funds. About one-third of the remainder goes to state and local governments in the form of grants-in-aid to carry out federally sponsored and supported programs or for unspecified purposes (revenue sharing).[9] One-third or more of that remainder goes to other institutions and individuals outside the federal government, also to carry out federally sponsored and supported programs and procurement. On the other side, this suggests that *only between 15 and 20 percent of federal spending is directed to activities that the federal government performs itself* (other than making and superintending payments to others). More than half of that amount is applied to the operations, maintenance, and personnel compensation of the armed forces. The corollary is that *considerably less than one-tenth of the federal budget is allotted to domestic activities that the federal government performs itself.* My guess is that the percentage of federal expenditures so allotted amounts to between 5 and 7 percent of the budget. A substantial proportion of this amount is, of course, used to administer and supervise funds granted or contracted to others outside the federal establishment.

II. THE GROWTH OF FEDERAL INVOLVEMENT, OVERT AND COVERT

At first blush, one might conclude from the data presented above that the federal government has not grown significantly in the last quarter century—indeed that in some respects it has been declining in relation to a growing population and economy. But this would be a misinterpretation. For example, while the federal work force has not grown, the number of persons whose pay is derived totally or largely from federal funds has increased enormously. In 1978, then–HEW Secretary Joseph A. Califano, Jr. stated that his department employed about 144,000 people but indirectly paid the salaries of 980,000 more in state and local governments, or about six times as many.[10] This ratio is probably high for the government as a whole. Yet, if one were to add to the state and local personnel paid from federal funds those in the private (and quasi-private) sectors who are principally dependent on federal contracts, the total would be far greater than direct federal hires. One recent survey estimated that there are about 8,000,000 nonfederal employees on federally supported payrolls.[11] This would be a ratio of nearly 4 to 1.

The expenditure figures are misleading in two opposite directions. First, they tend to overstate federal activities since one-half of them are simply transfers, mostly of money, from one set of pockets to another. They exhaust few resources, no human effort beyond those involved in collecting the revenues and paying them out. A large portion of them are from trust funds, which until a decade ago were not even included in the federal budget. On the other hand, federal expenditures are for several reasons inadequate indicators of what the government gets done (or tries to get done) and of its impact upon the society and the economy. Some of its programs with their accompanying conditions are very nearly costless to the government but entail enormous costs and, one hopes, benefits to the society or sectors thereof. These include regulatory activities, tax expenditures, loan guarantees, and public or quasi-public enterprises, all of which are discussed below.

The use and the extent of all of these tools have grown enormously in recent years—even as federally performed domestic operations virtually stood still. Few new policies and programs failed to rely upon other governments or institutions in the private sector for a major part or all of their execution. The extension of federal interest and intervention into the nooks and crannies of our economic, social, cultural, and even personal lives seems almost unlimited. And most of this is being done through others, not strictly a part of the federal government itself. The growth of federal influence defies precise quantitative measurement, but there can be no question that it has been pervasive—unmatched in American history except in time of major war or the disastrous depression of the 1930s. Some of the types of federal involvement are discussed briefly below.

Income Support

The largest category of federal expenditures consists of payments, mainly, but not exclusively in cash, to individuals and families for whom no direct service or products *for the government* are expected.[12] If income support payments made through state and local governments and private institutions are included (as for Medicaid, housing, and public assistance), the total would be nearly half of all federal outlays. A large share of this amount is from funds held in trust by the government, part of which have previously been contributed by the recipients and their employers in taxes and retirement contributions. The government has little or no direction over how and for what purpose much of this money is ultimately spent. This is true of social security, unemployment insurance, pension and retirement payments, and others. But there are important exceptions: Medicare and Medicaid for health services; food stamps for food; housing subsidies for housing; and so forth.

Federal responsibilities in these areas include:

- through law and regulation, devising and promulgating the rules of the game: what kinds of people are entitled to or eligible for payments, when and how much;

- delivering or monitoring the delivery of the funds or, in some cases, payments in kind or services; this may, in some instances, involve interpretation of the law and regulation;

- accounting, auditing, and investigating to assure that the funds or goods and services are provided in proper amounts to the proper people;

- evaluating the effects of such payments, and then recommending changes in laws and regulations.

Most payments in this category are based upon entitlements: those who qualify under the law and regulations are entitled to receive them. There is presumably little administrative discretion except in interpretation and application of the rules as they apply to individual recipients or classes of recipients.[13] Budgeting amounts only to estimating how many will be entitled and for how much. That is to say that the amounts are largely uncontrollable in the budget process. And movements downward (not upward) are extremely difficult even through legislation. The elimination or reduction of most entitlements, once established, would be politically, morally, and, in many cases, legally repugnant.

Contracts and Grants

Contracts and grants differ from income support because, in the main, they are intended to contribute to the accomplishment of federal programs considered to be in the national interest, in whole or in part. There is usually a *quid pro quo*; that is, the government anticipates that something will be done, or has been done, in return for its payments. The "something" may be very specific (building airports or highways, designing a nuclear reactor, research on cancer cells) or very general (relieving fiscal stringency of local governments, unspecified aid to an underdeveloped country, basic research in uncharted areas). The nature and degree of federal control varies widely but is not usually as immediate and authoritative as it is in connection with "in-house" undertakings. In fact, the extent of federal initiative, involvement, intrusion, regulation, and penalties comprehend some of the most difficult and controversial issues in America today. They involve not alone state and local jurisdictions but also foreign governments, international organizations, private enterprises both profit and nonprofit, and even individual persons.

Obviously, the growing reliance upon outsiders to carry out federal programs greatly complicates the problem of accountability for the expenditure of public money. This problem is further aggravated when, and to the extent that, the government delegates with its funds responsibilities to determine or modify projects and programs—i.e., to make federal policy. Examples of this are abundant among many types of grants and contracts. Indeed, in some fields it is not uncommon for the government to draw contracts and to make grants for the specific purpose of developing or changing public policy.

Regulation

A substantial part of the growth of federal influence is a consequence of the extension of federal contracts and grants, described above, most of which involved some degree of federal regulation of hitherto private or state/local activities. But a good deal of federal involvement has been developed in areas without the "rabbit" of subsidies and contracts. Most federal regulation in the past has been directed to industries considered to have a particular national interest: railways, airlines, food, drugs, radio and TV, and others. The more recent innovations in regulation have not applied to specific industries but to enterprises in general, not only industrial but nonprofit and even the governments themselves. They include, for example, equal opportunity in employment, environmental protection, use of energy, occupational health, consumer products, and many others. Even as there is pressure for deregulation in some areas, there is a growing demand for more regulation in others. There are now 58 regulatory agencies including 18 independent commissions. They issue about 7,000 rules and policy statements each year. The cost of regulation to the government itself is relatively minor in budgetary terms, probably about 1 percent of the budget; but its costs to others in the society at large are, if not precisely estimable, certainly enormous. Recent guesses range between $50 billion and $150 billion a year.

Tax Expenditures

The obverse and more positive side of regulation is inducement: providing incentives for people to do what the federal government deems desirable. Among the means are credits, deductions, and exemptions of various kinds from federal taxes, mainly the income taxes. Tax expenditures (though not so labeled) have almost always been with us. But only recently have they been widely recognized as a major instrument of specific public policies, as in encouraging investment, environmental protection, home-ownership, indirect subsidies to state and local governments, energy conservation, and many others.

Tax expenditures are not considered in the regular budget process except peripherally and are not included in the budget as expenditures. However, they are now estimated to amount to about $170 billion, equivalent to nearly 30 percent of budgetary expenditures.[14]

Loans and Loan Guarantees

The federal government has long been heavily involved in credit activities, both as lender and borrower. As lender and guarantor of loans, its outstanding credit has grown almost geometrically in the last decade—from under $200 billion in 1970 to almost $600 billion in 1980.[15] The largest part of this growth has been in the form of loan guarantees whereby the government commits itself to secure a lender of money for a federal purpose against the possible default of a borrower. Unlike most direct loans by federal agencies, loan guarantees do not enter into the budget except and until actual default by the borrower. The principal purpose of loan guarantees was to support and encourage housing programs, but they have recently been extended to a wide variety of uses: international assistance, trade, energy, railroads, education, small business, New York City, and now the Chrysler Corporation. Total credit advanced by the government is now running about $125 billion per year and is increasing. The largest part of it is in the form of loan guarantees. Outstanding guaranteed loans, including those of government-sponsored enterprises, amounted to about $300 billion in 1979.[16]

The Twilight Zones[17]

An increasing number of organizations have been established to carry out federal objectives which lie somewhere in between the sectors traditionally defined as public and private. They are, in widely varying degrees, independent of the government with respect to their ownership, financing, policies and programs, internal organization, and control. Many of those established in the last 30 years are largely independent of the federal budget process and normal personnel controls. There are long historical precedents for such institutions: the Federal Reserve System, Federal Land Banks, and many others. More recently, there are COMSAT, AMTRAK, CONRAIL, Corporation for Public Broadcasting, Postal Service, Legal Services Corporation to mention a few. A major one recently established is the Synthetic Fuels Corporation.

A "twilight zone" of a somewhat different kind is that in which the federal government shares its activities with state and local governments like the Advisory Commission on Intergovernmental Relations, a variety of regional commissions, and others. Still another kind of "twilight" is a combination of the two above which bridges both the public-private and the intergovernmental divisions. Examples are the community action agencies of the poverty program and the health systems agencies. Finally, one should mention a vast array of quasi-public organizations established by or for state and local as well as the federal government to carry out public programs like community development, Medicaid and Medicare, and CETA.

The justification and the rhetoric for "twilight" organizations like these are various: to eliminate partisan political interventions; to free them of normal federal controls with regard to budget, personnel and other controls, like personnel ceilings; to protect the interests of clienteles; and others. But one effect is to reduce or at least make questionable the legal controls of the president and also of the Congress over their activities.

III. A TRULY NEW PUBLIC ADMINISTRATION

The problems that the federal government is now called upon to address and try to resolve are more numerous, more complex, more interrelated than ever before in history. It has responded to them piecemeal through fragmented institutions and practices, conceived with almost unbelievable inventiveness. These have added new and complicated twists to old tools, like grants and contracts and regulations and tax deductions to the point that these kinds of devices are more important in the big picture than the things the government does for itself. Some of them are very expensive, far more so than was anticipated when they were begun—like income support programs, grants-in-aid, and procurement and other contracts. Others—like regulatory activities, tax expenditures, and loan guarantees—seem almost costless to the government. In most cases, their inexpensiveness is an illusion.

The extent, the scope, and the detail of federal intervention in other sectors of the society magnify the possibilities of corruption, inequality, resentment, dissent, complaint, and consequently, of politics, even in the carrying out of what might appear to be mundane tasks. They also involve federal administration up and down the line in issues that are highly technical or deeply ethical or sometimes (as in biomedical research or new weaponry) both. Federal law and regulation makers and administrators must now confront human problems once handled by local governments or the schools, the churches, private businesses, charitable organizations, families—or not handled at all.

Distribution of Federal Sector Expenditures by Category

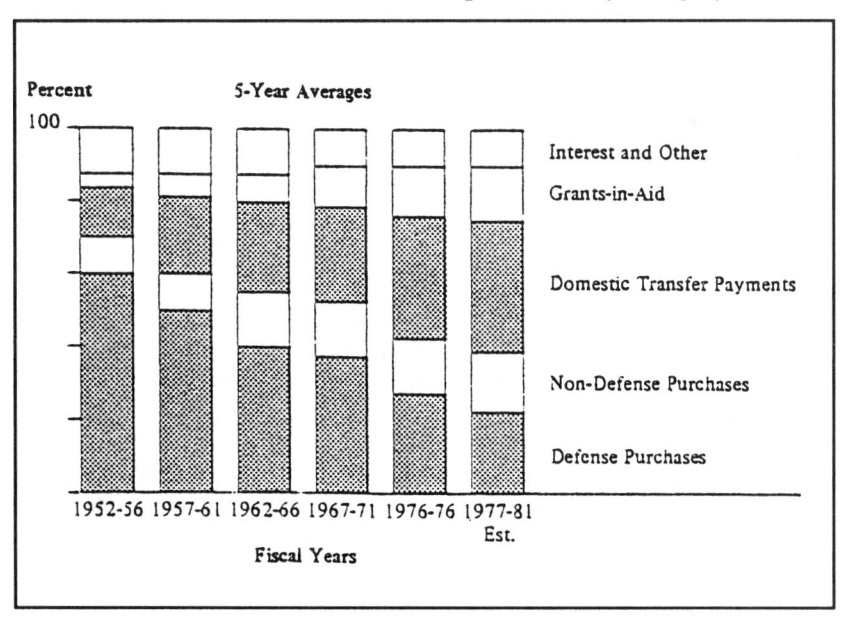

THE CHANGING RESPONSIBILITIES AND TACTICS OF FEDERAL GOVERNMENT

The ways in which the federal government—and to a lesser extent subnational governments—have absorbed and accommodated to growing responsibilities have been largely uncoordinated, often contradictory, and, viewed overall, sloppy. Yet the tremendous growth in federal influence in the society over the last three decades has been very nearly a miracle, for it was done with only moderate increases in federal expenditures in relation to the total economy, almost none during the decade of the 1970s. It was done with a slight decline in the proportion of persons on the federal payroll. It was done while the operative activities of the national government itself were in fact declining substantially in proportion both to the budget and to the economy as a whole.

These massive changes in the *content* of what the government undertakes to have done and in the *means* by which it undertakes to have it done have enormous consequences for the *content* and the *means* of public administration, the principal and indispensable arm of implementation. Some of the operational implications of these developments for public administration are:

- Greatly increased reliance upon indirect administration through outsiders (third parties), less upon direct management by insiders;

which means

- more reliance upon negotiation, collaboration inducements, persuasion, rewards, and penalties in the private and subnational governmental sectors, less on immediate direction and control;

- extension and intensification of influence and pressure from interest groups (including public interest groups) on federal policy and administration; and increase in the numbers and clout of single purpose interest groups;

- increasing possibilities of political pressures arising from decisions (in policies, regulations, and their application) at lower levels of administration and appealed through interest groups, regional groups, congressmen, outside individuals, and organizations to cabinet and White House levels, the president and Congress;

- declining usefulness of the budget process as a tool for directing, integrating, and controlling governmental operations, because:
  - most governmental expenditures are committed in prior years, legally or politically;
  - most significant programs which cause present or future expenditures are decided on an *ad hoc* basis, independent of the budget process;
  - some of the most important tools and organizations for carrying out public policy are totally or principally outside the budget process: regulations, tax expenditures, loan guarantees, and others;
- greater concern and involvement in the administration of personnel who are paid from U.S. funds but on the roles of organizations outside immediate federal control;
- increasing legalization and judicialization of administrative decision making and execution, with increasing involvement by the courts.

Federal Sector Expenditures as a Percent of GNP

Description	1949-51 Average Actual	1959-61 Average Actual	1969-71 Average Actual	1979-81 Average Estimate
Defense purchases	5.5	9.3	7.8	4.7
Nondefense purchases	2.2	1.8	2.3	2.6
Domestic transfer payments	3.3	4.3	5.9	9.1
Foreign transfer payments	1.5	0.4	0.2	0.2
Grants-in-aid to state and local governments	0.8	1.4	2.4	3.4
Net interest paid	1.5	1.3	1.4	1.9
Subsidies less current surplus of government enterprises	0.3	0.6	0.6	0.4
Total expenditures	15.2	19.0	20.6	22.1

Source: *Special Analyses, Budget of the United States Government*, 1981, 52-53.

THE CHANGING RESPONSIBILITIES AND TACTICS OF FEDERAL GOVERNMENT

The national government is becoming a great and enveloping super-conglomerate with growing influence on the economy and the society. Whether this development is desirable, or the extent to which it is desirable, and whether it is reversible are questions beyond the scope of this article. I address two more immediate problems for public administration. The first is the *coordination* of public programs and the *simplification* of the means whereby they may be carried out. Some scholars have extolled complexity in public administration and legislation; it is a challenge, it is fun. But it is at least possible that complexity may grow beyond the bounds of the most brilliant human minds. I suspect that it already has. One would be a dreamer to imagine that public administrators by themselves could reverse the current complexity. But surely they could, in their management of little or big programs, influence those programs so that they are at least roughly consonant with other programs, with undertakings that are not organizationally related, and with the benefit of the society as a whole.

The second has to do with that will-o-the-wisp, *accountability*. It must be generally agreed that a major requirement of representative government is that the officials who decide and act for the citizenry be held accountable for their actions. This was a fairly simple concept—though never very easy to ensure—when one was concerned simply with legality, honesty, and correctness of actions by persons under direct electoral or hierarchical control. It has become far more difficult as the concept has extended to the efficiency and effectiveness of performance in terms of governmental purposes by organizations and persons outside of the government. The perspectives on goals of given programs and projects of outsiders almost inevitably differ in some degree from those of federal officials. The nature of operations, of accounting and record-keeping and reporting likewise differ, as do the criteria for evaluating results. To what extent should and can the federal government intrude and impose upon other institutions—other governments, private businesses, universities, individuals—its own customary requirements for purposes of maintaining accountability?

The values associated with public accountability have long been competitors of other values in our society, such as: the sovereignty of foreign nations; states' rights; local autonomy and self-government; the free-market economy; private initiative and experimentation; freedom of information; personal privacy; freedom of inquiry and academic freedom; avoidance of conflicts of interest; national security; and others. The explosive growth in reliance on institutions outside the government to carry out its purposes and even to make its policy has intensified this competition. In many areas we are in need of fresh insights, new accommodations, and techniques to maintain an adequate degree of accountability without violating these other widely held values.

* * * * *

Many years ago, Dean Rusk, then secretary of state, is reported to have admonished foreign service officers that they should know everything there is to know.[18] This obviously impossible prescription nonetheless bears a useful message for public administrators of the present and the future. Judgment without knowledge is no more valuable than knowledge without judgment. Whether judgment can be taught, except through personal observation and experience, is doubtful. But knowledge, by definition, can be acquired, and teaching can help. The content and nature of public administration depends upon the content and nature of the government it serves. In the last generation, the federal government has experienced a sea change: it is itself *doing* less but *influencing* far more. It has at the same time become far more dependent upon institutions outside itself.

It seems to me doubtful that many of us in public administration have kept sufficiently abreast of the problems and implications of the massive changes in American government—in our research, our literature, our teaching. The nature of public management itself has changed; it must look outward more, inward relatively less. A useful base might be an inventory and topology of the almost limitless array of devices that have already been tried by government in pursuit of goals, followed by assessments of the advantages and disadvantages, the success and failures of each major one. We need to know more about how best to deliver human services and benefits because they are large, they are growing, and they are not going away. Likewise, we need to know more about the direction, management, and effects of devices to utilize and to modify the private society and other governments: regulations, taxes and tax expenditures, loans and loan guarantees, contracts for goods and services, including procurement, quasi-governmental enterprises, and others. Most of these fall beyond the limits of the traditional controls, budget and personnel, we have inherited from our forebears.

Most important of all is that our top public executives bring to their work an understanding of the relations and the interdependence of the public sector and the private, and of one level of government with others, both above and below. It would be helpful if there were some up-to-date social philosophy which might rationalize where we are and where we are going. Some have said we are approaching socialism, but not in the ways contemplated by Karl Marx; others, that we are approaching fascism, but not in ways utilized by Mussolini. Certainly there is a degree of interinvolvement—mutual intrusion if you prefer—of institutions seldom before experienced in American history. And public administrators at every level should be aware of it.

Frederick C. Mosher

NOTES

1. It is not my intent to present an exhaustive analysis of trends in expenditures and personnel, nor to offer prescriptive judgments as to the desirability of those trends. They are summarized here only as introductory evidence of the fundamental shift in the *content* and *methods* of governmental operations. There have been a number of articles in recent years on spending and employment whose findings are generally in agreement with mine. These include, particularly, Shariff, Zahid, "How Big is Big Government?," *Social Policy*, 8, (March/April 1978), 22–27; and Thomas, John Clayton, "The Growth of American Public Expenditures: Recent Trends and Their Implications," *Public Administration Review*, 40, 2, (March/April 1980), 160–65.

    My principal data sources have been the various documents of the federal budget for fiscal year 1981: *The Budget of the United States Government*, *The Budget in Brief*, and *Special Analyses*.

2. In fiscal year (FY) 1960, it was 20.6 percent; in FY 1979, it was 19.9 percent. Its peak in that period was 22.3 percent in 1968; its nadir in 1974 was 18.8 percent. That 20-year span comprehended all of the Johnson Great Society programs and their supplements as well as the Vietnam War. See Pechman, Joseph A. and Robert W. Hartman, "The 1980 Budget and the Budget Outlook" in *Setting National Priorities: The 1980 Budget* (The Brookings Institution, 1979), 26.

3. These data are drawn from the national income accounts as reported in the *Economic Report of the President* (Washington, D.C.: U.S. Government Printing Office, 1980), appendix B, table B-1, 203. They do not include total expenditures of the Postal Service and other governmental enterprises, only their surpluses or deficits that affect the federal budget.

4. *Special Analyses, op. cit.*, p. 288 and previous years.

5. For 1947, 1957, and 1967, U.S. Department of Commerce, Bureau of the Census, *Historical Statistics of the United States* (Washington, D.C.: U.S. Government Printing Office, 1975), 1141. For 1979, *Special Analyses, op. cit.*, 279.

6. Not including commercial-type organizations for which only annual surpluses and deficits are included in the budget.

7. The only source I can find for this kind of data is the "Object Class Analysis: Budget for Fiscal Year 1981," U.S. Office of Management and Budget, January 1980.

8. National Science Foundation, *Federal Funds for Research, Development, and Other Scientific Activities*, fiscal years 1975, 1976, 1977, NSF 77-301, Vol. 25 (Washington, D.C.: U.S. Government Printing Office).

9. As indicated earlier, more than one-third of this amount consists of indirect transfer payments to individuals, paid through and administered by state and local governments.

10. In his remarks before the Economics Club of Chicago, Illinois, 20 April 1978.

11. Blumenthal, Barbara, "Uncle Sam's Army of Invisible Employees," *National Journal*, 5 May 1979, 730-33.

12. Payments of this kind are widely associated with the "welfare state." They are redistributive and only indirectly productive. Some have alleged that their aim and effect are to equalize income and wealth in the society. The economic and social impact of such redistribution is beyond the scope of this article. The evidence that I have seen suggests that, despite the fact that some categories of the poor benefit, income support payments as a whole have not materially influenced the distribution of wealth one way or the other; rather, as Shariff notes (*op. cit.*, p. 26), they have contributed to the "stabilization of the existing pattern of inequalities."

13. Where the law and rules are not exhaustively explicit to cover every conceivable contingency, there is discretion in interpretation for unusual cases; this amounts to the making of new policy.

14. See Joseph A. Pechman (ed.), *Setting National Priorities: The 1980 Budget*, Brookings Institution, 1979, Appendix B.

15. These figures include loans and guarantees by both budget and off-budget federal agencies and by government-sponsored enterprises.

16. The data in this section are drawn from the *Budget* for 1981, pp. 17ff. and the *Special Analyses* of the U.S. Budget, 1981, *op. cit.*, F.

17. I am indebted to Harold Seidman for this term. (See his *Politics, Position and Power* (Oxford University Press, 3rd ed., 1980) p. 277ff.) For a recent and perceptive analysis of the nature, extent, and problems of organizations in the "twilight zone," see Musolf, Lloyd D. and Seidman, Harold, "The Blurred Boundaries of Public Administration," *Public Administration Review*, 40, 2, March/April 1980, 124–130.

18. In a speech to the American Foreign Services Association.

CHAPTER SIX

A Tale of Two Agencies (The General Accounting Office and the Office of Management and Budget): The Agencies and Their Changing Milieu*

FREDERICK C. MOSHER

> This power over the purse may, in fact, be regarded as the most complete and effectual weapon with which any constitution can arm the immediate representatives of the people.
>
> JAMES MADISON, 1778
>
> Energy in the Executive is a leading character in the definition of good government.
>
> ALEXANDER HAMILTON, 1778

On 10 June 1921, President Warren G. Harding signed into law the Budget and Accounting Act (Public Law 67-13), which gave the nation an executive budget system and two new agencies, the

---

Reprinted by permission of Louisiana State University Press from A Tale of Two Agencies (A Comparative Analysis of the General Accounting Office and the Office of Management and Budget), by Frederick C. Mosher. ©1984 by Louisiana State University Press.

Bureau of the Budget (BOB), and the General Accounting Office (GAO). The agencies were twins, born at the same time to the same parents (Congress and the president) following the same nine-year pregnancy. They were conceived in the same social milieu, and their purposes, as originally envisioned, were roughly consonant. But they were not identical twins, far from it. Most of the responsibilities of one (the GAO) were in fact very old before it was born, whereas the other (BOB) was truly a newcomer. Even ten years after their birth, the former was 40 times the size of the latter, and it remains, after 60 years, about nine times as large. Their personalities came to differ as much as their sizes and other physical characteristics. And over the six decades of their growth and maturation, like a lot of other twins, the two were only in rather limited ways friendly and respectful toward each other.

The General Accounting Office was basically the product of a simple transfer of certain powers, responsibilities, and resources from an executive department (Treasury) to independent and congressional status. A few new responsibilities were added—such as the supervision of agency accounting systems—but the main GAO mission was a continuation of that given the Treasury Department by the First Congress of the Republic in 1789: to assure that the financial transactions of the United States government were proper, accurate, and legal.[1]

That mission was not greatly altered by the 1921 law; its executor simply became independent and partially legislative rather than executive, a situation that led to bitter controversy over the first half of GAO's history. In fact, its powers have not been greatly changed since 1921, but the original functions and the methods by which they are exercised have undergone two revolutions and are virtually unrecognizable today. GAO has become a large, pragmatic research organization, studying the organizations, policies, programs, operations, and effectiveness of the government and issuing reports and recommendations thereon.

From its beginning, the Bureau of the Budget, whose name was changed in 1970 to the Office of Management and Budget (OMB), has been one of the principal support agencies directly responsible to the president, usually the major one with a permanent staff and the only one, other than the White House staff,

Frederick C. Mosher

with generalized jurisdiction.[2] This was true even when it was officially and physically a part of the Department of the Treasury between 1921 and 1939. From its beginning it had responsibility for putting together, publishing, and supervising the *Budget of the United States* on behalf of the president. Almost from the start it was also concerned with the coordination and clearance of proposed legislation and agency comments and presidential action thereon. Since the late 1930s, it has been variously involved in questions of management and organization of the executive branch, but the nature and extent of such involvement have fluctuated and remain a major debating point. Many other functions have come and gone, and a few have returned. Perceptions of BOB/OMB have varied all the way from one of a simple budget-accounting agency with exclusive interest in numbers of dollars to another view that it is the general staff of the president, involved on his behalf in every major problem and policy of the executive branch.

The BOB/OMB has long—indeed from its very beginning—been regarded as one of the most powerful institutions in the federal government. The record of the General Accounting Office has been less consistent in this regard, and there is less agreement about it among observers today. But that it has had influence back to and before the New Deal and that its influence has been growing over the last 20 to 25 years can hardly be questioned. Its power is less immediate and less clear, particularly to officials within the executive branch. But it is one of the few major institutional tools of the Congress. And except for the unusual prominence of OMB and its director during the first year of the Reagan administration, its products—testimony, reports, recommendations—reach the media and the public far more frequently than do those of the OMB. Its indirect and long-range impact may be very great indeed, even if immeasurable.

There has been a considerable literature about BOB and OMB, mainly articles and brief studies, but rather few books. Until quite recently, there was little literature about the GAO, which publishes an enormous amount of literature, but not about itself.[3] It is interesting and also symptomatic that no one to my knowledge has undertaken to describe and analyze these two agencies, the twins, *together*: their histories within the temporal contexts of

American society and its problems; their organizations and personnel; their relationships with the president and his executive office, with the Congress, with federal agencies both off- and on-budget, and with each other. Few scholars who have studied BOB/OMB have looked at the GAO, and vice versa. Very possibly, students of government have carried the separation of powers too far into their own research. Until about 15 years ago, there was rather little interchange in personnel among the leaders of the two agencies, so that few could comment about their observations and experiences in both. This has been partly corrected recently, mainly by the movement of high officials of BOB/OMB into GAO, though seldom the reverse.[4] So we may before long benefit from their insights about the two agencies. In the meantime, I undertake in this study to summarize the parallel origins and development of the two and to offer some reflections on the influences that affected that development, their likenesses and differences, their problems, and most of all, their significance in the American system of government.

In some ways, and apart from the obvious differences between the presidency and the Congress, these agencies are the most striking yet enduring institutional expressions of the separation between the executive and legislative powers in the national government.[5] Both grew out of an issue as to presidential-congressional powers with respect to finances that has been festering ever since the Constitution was drafted in 1787 and that even then had precedents in British and colonial times. The Bureau of the Budget was set up as, and has always been regarded as, primarily a *presidential* agency. But not exclusively so. Although expected from the beginning to report directly to the president, it was originally a bureau in the Department of the Treasury. Even after it became a central element in the Executive Office of the President in 1939, its dependence on the president was not total; Congress continued to control its resources, to a varying extent its policies, and its powers and responsibilities. In 1973, when an irate Congress insisted that the director and deputy director of the OMB be appointed subject to confirmation by the Senate, that action further diminished the immediate dependence of the agency upon the president.

Frederick C. Mosher

On the other hand, the General Accounting Office was conceived and established as primarily a congressional agency or at least as one outside the executive branch. It was given independent powers for which it accounts only to the deity and most of which it seldom exercises—at least in the last several decades. It is dependent on the Congress for its resources, powers, and responsibilities, though it has long had rather unusual freedom in planning and directing its work. It was not until 1945 that Congress in legislation declared that it was "part of the legislative branch."[6] Its head and his first assistant, the comptroller general and his deputy, are appointed by the president, subject to confirmation by the Senate. But unlike the director of OMB and virtually all other presidential appointments in the executive branch, they have long, fixed terms of 15 years and are practically irremovable. None has ever been removed against his will. This means among other things that, once appointed, a comptroller general is unlikely to be subjected to official pressure from a president or others in his executive office. Some comptrollers general in the past have deliberately avoided contacts with high officials in the executive branch, and their contacts with presidents have been infrequent.

The contrasting conditions of their appointment and removal have led to astonishing differences between budget directors and comptrollers general in terms of lengths of service and continuity. In their first 60 years (from 1 July 1921) there were 25 directors of the budget, each with an average tenure of about two-and-a-half years. In the same period, there were a total of five comptrollers general, each with an average tenure of about 11 years. Every incoming president of a different political party from his predecessor has almost immediately appointed a new budget director, and most of them have appointed one to three succeeding budget directors. Only President Coolidge never appointed a new budget director. In this 60-year span, only four of 11 presidents (not including President Reagan) had an opportunity to appoint even one comptroller general: Presidents Harding, Roosevelt (who appointed two), Eisenhower, and Johnson. The vast differences in length of tenure have had a major impact on the nature of the two agencies, their political postures, their adaptation to change, and their internal modes of operating.

These two agencies work primarily for two of the most political institutions in this nation or in any nation: the president and the Congress of the United States. There are many connotations to the word *political*—party, interest group, policy, ideology—and I refer to all of them. But the laurels of both agencies have rested for much of their histories on their neutrality, their objectivity, and their professional competence. Most of their staffs have from the beginning been career employees who could survive partisan or ideological changes without threat to their jobs. But the balance between neutrality and responsiveness to political change is a fragile one, requiring appropriate protective legislation and sensitive management at the top. For both agencies, though in different ways, this has been a recurring problem. It is a central theme of this study.

THE CHANGING CONTEXT AS THEY GREW

It requires no particular originality or insight to observe that the six decades since 1921 have witnessed tremendous changes in the world, in the society, and in government, and these changes have been paralleled or followed in these two agencies. Indeed, it is remarkable and a bit unfortunate that the titles of the comptroller general and his GAO remain as they were at the beginning for they are, and were then, misleading indicators of what they do. It took nearly half a century before BOB's name was changed to OMB, which some people today think is also a misnomer. In fact, the nature and the functions of GAO have been more completely transformed since 1921 than have those of BOB/OMB. The latter's responsibilities have always been tied to the budget and the processes utilized in its formulation and execution. Although different presidents have used the agency in different ways, it has always been close to the presidency and derives most of its influence and clout from that office.

Many of the most basic changes in these two agencies were responses, sometimes slow, to changes in the society and its values, in technology, in the role and responsibilities of American governments and particularly the federal government itself, in the economy, and in our international relations. In other words, the changes within the agencies often resulted form forces and conditions exogenous to them. To a considerable degree, therefore, their evolution offers parallels and some similarities. Both grew out of the same movements—scientific management and economy and efficiency, which from the turn of the century provided the driving forces of reform in many state and local governments. The drafting and passage of the 1921 act probably owed much to the financial experience and consequences of World War I. Financial mismanagement of the war was suspected. By earlier standards, federal expenditures and taxes were high, and the federal debt was enormous. These were the basic arguments for the Budget and Accounting Act of 1921; its rationale was thrift, efficiency, legality, and strict central control.

It would clearly not be feasible in a few sentences to describe the myriad changes since 1921 that have influenced federal operations generally or the activities of the two agencies here under consideration. But it may be useful to spotlight a few of them, some widely known, some less familiar. A first category has to do with the *dimensions* of federal operations. In the six decades from 1922, the first year in which the Budget and Accounting Act was fully operative, to 1981:

> the U.S. population, which the government is designed to serve, doubled (from 110 million to 225 million);

> the gross national product (GNP) multiplied by nearly 40 times (from $74 billion to $2,844 billion); a large part of this increase was due to decline in the value of the dollar; in terms of dollars of constant value, the increase was by about seven times;

> the amount of federal outlays (unadjusted) grew from $3.8 billion to $663 billion, or by about 175 times; in dollars of constant value, the increase would have been by more than 35 times;

> the proportion of federal budget outlays to GNP grew from 5 to 23 percent.

The original practices of both the BOB and GAO were directed to details: in the case of BOB, to individual items (known as objects) with their numbers and prices, and in that of GAO, to individual transactions to be audited. For example, in 1947, GAO was called upon to audit over 40 million vouchers, 260 million postal money orders, and 770,000 claims, and to reconcile 490 million checks. Were similar financial systems in place today, the comparable numbers would be beyond the imagination. The original central budgeting and auditing systems were doomed simply by scale.

One effect of the enormous growth in federal activity was to force a considerable degree of decentralization from the central agencies to the operating departments, their bureaus, and other units. One of the purposes of the original Bureau of the Budget was to centralize direction, review, and control of the budget in a single body, accountable to the president. The General Accounting Office inherited from the comptroller and the auditors of the Treasury Department one of the most highly centralized systems imaginable for reviewing, auditing, and settling financial transactions. However successful the centralizing effort was in the early years of BOB/OMB, the sheer dimensions of federal activity have necessitated that the great bulk of the work on the budget, on administrative management, and on other activities be performed in the operating agencies. Much the same is true of the auditing and program evaluation activities of the GAO. The work of both agencies must necessarily depend upon management by selection (of the unusual, the nonroutine), and their effectiveness depends in part upon the information and the wisdom with which they select the crucial and the exceptional.

A cluster of factors that have had enormous impact upon these two agencies include the tremendous enlargement of the *scope* and *variety* of federal undertakings and the *complexity* and *specialization* that have necessarily accompanied it. Scope can be described in many ways. The federal government is now involved in one or many respects with every person (including noncitizens), every institution and organization, and almost every activity in the country. Its assumption of responsibilities for the young, the aging, the poor, the handicapped, the sick, minorities, and a great many other groups of citizens during and since the 1930s now consumes nearly half of its financial outlays. It is heavily involved in fields and problems heretofore the exclusive province of states, local governments, schools, universities, industries, families—or not taken care of at all. These include energy, the environment, outer space, the resources of the oceans, abortion, the arts, civil rights, the aged and the children, pornography, drugs, alcohol, health care, housing, crime, and others almost without limit. The federal government has become the principal sponsor and supporter of research and development in most scientific fields. It is by far the biggest borrower and also the biggest lender in the nation. It is involved in a variety of relationships with every nation in the world, with most of the international organizations, and with all of the 50 states, the territories, the cities, the counties, and most of the school and other districts of the nation.

Many of these federal activities require a high degree of professional and scientific learning and experience, and cumulatively these specializations within the government comprehend almost every nook and cranny of human knowledge today. The effectiveness with which a central agency such as BOB/OMB can contribute to the planning, budgeting, and managing of activities in such highly variegated and specialized fields without a vast assortment of its own specialists in problematic. So is that of GAO in its efforts to appraise management and evaluate results of federal programs against their costs. This growing phenomenon of specialization raises questions not only as to the degree to which the central agencies should attempt to match the specializations of federal agencies in their own staffing but also of the extent and depth to which they should seek to penetrate the operations and appraise the results of highly technical programs.

The growth in scope of federal involvement has been complicated by the growing realization of interdependence and interrelationships. No longer are the convenient divisions of the past inviolable, the divisions between what is foreign and what is purely national; what is federal and what is state or local; what is public and what is private; what is legislative, what is executive, and what is judicial; what is defense and what is domestic; what is education and what is health or drugs or crime. The graying of these once familiar boundaries has complicated the organization and operations of the government generally. It has particularly aggravated the difficulties of coordinating related and overlapping programs, the appraisal of results against costs, and the whole area of accountability—all central to the responsibilities of OMB and GAO.

Another area of basic change for both of these agencies and indeed for the entire federal establishment has been the virtual revolution in the *modes* and *means* whereby the government carries out its programs. During and before the 1920s, most of what the federal government was responsible for it did for itself with its own personnel and facilities. The New Deal and later the Great Society and subsequent programs relied heavily on nonfederal organizations—state and local governments, quasi-public organizations, universities and other nonprofit organizations, and even private businesses—to carry out operations presumably in the national interest and financed in whole or part by federal funds. Furthermore, a large part of what the federal government now does and buys in terms of services, equipment and supplies, research and development, and even planning and policy-making is actually produced or performed by individuals and organizations outside of itself. This is why, in the last generation, roughly since the Korean War, though federal expenditures have grown, there has little increase in direct federal employment. At the present time more than one-half of all federal outlays consists of direct payments to individuals and families for their support and for interest on the national debt. About one-third consists of payments to state and local units for grants-in-aid and payments to nongovernmental organizations, at home and abroad, in return for goods and services to be produced and provided by them for federal purposes. The remainder, about one-sixth of the total, is for services and other costs directly incurred for federal operations. Of this last category of federal operations, about two-thirds is for national defense. This means that only about 5 percent of the total federal budget goes to domestic operations that are carried out by the government itself. Indeed, the Reagan budget for 1983 showed only 4 percent for direct, nondefense federal operations.

The impact of this development upon the federal budget and financial management generally has been great. It means, among many other things, that a substantial part of the annual budget is beyond discretionary decision during the appropriation process because it is committed in law or contract in prior years.[7] It means, too, that when the government plans, projects, and budgets its programs and outlays, it is dealing in large part with operations and with things that will be performed and produced by nonfederal agencies, public and private, foreign and domestic; that is, by organizations and individuals beyond the immediate hierarchical control of the federal government itself. Budgeting today is largely a matter of predicting what others, outside the government, are entitled to receive from, or do in behalf of, federal programs. Furthermore, there are a good many potentially leaky straws twixt the cup and the lip. This introduces new complications to the problems of appraising program effectiveness against costs, or in other words to the problems of accountability in its broadest sense. How far is it appropriate and permissible for a federal agency to audit or investigate the affairs of foreign governments, international organizations, state and local governments, private businesses, universities, and even individuals to ascertain whether they have used their federal funds legally and efficiently in pursuit of federally mandated purposes?

Another important change in the modes and means of operations has been the increasing reliance for carrying out national goals upon tools that have no impact or very slight impact upon budgetary outlays. Among these are the increasing numbers of off-budget government and mixed ownership enterprises such as the Postal Service, AMTRAK, CONRAIL, COMSAT, and the Corporation for Public Broadcasting. Another device is the use of credits, deductions, and exemptions of various kinds from federal taxes, now commonly known as tax expenditures, for the purpose of carrying out federal policies. Another is the guaranteeing of loans to encourage or support housing, trade, energy, railroads, agriculture, education, community development, small business, ailing cities (such as New York), and ailing corporations (such as Lockheed and Chrysler). Finally, mention should be made of the recently exploding use of regulations to carry out federal policy in both private and public realms of activity. The cost to the government of regulation of others is relatively minor, but its costs to the economy as a whole, though immeasurable, are certainly substantial.

A final type of change to be mentioned here has been the development of *technology*, which has virtually revolutionized the processes of financial management. In 1921, a great deal of the work of building and executing budgets and of auditing of vouchers and accounts was done by pencil on paper, augmented here and there by typewriters and telephones. Adding machines, punch-card systems, computers were still in the future. Today, most of the spadework of financial management is computerized, individual vouchers are seldom seen by auditors, accounts are consolidated and retained in memory banks, funds are electronically transferred, and alternative programs and their costs are programmed and calculated on machines. Such developments, whose invention was largely extrinsic to these two agencies themselves, have made budgeting, accounting, and auditing infinitely more complex. But in light of the growth in dimensions and scope and ramifications of federal undertakings, they have made them possible. The jobs could not be done with the tools that were available in 1921.

THEIR STAGES OF DEVELOPMENT

In response to these tremendous changes of federal dimensions, scope, modes of operating, and technology, the two agencies changed, but probably at a somewhat slower pace than the changes that were going on around them. In general, GAO's pace of change was slower than that of BOB/OMB, at least until quite recently. Thus, their changes, though roughly parallel in nature, were not coterminous. Over the 60-year period, GAO went through three fairly definable phases; BOB/OMB, three or possibly four.

The first phase for both agencies was generally but not totally consonant with the letter and intent of the 1921 law as perceived by the legislators who had passed it. The emphases during this phase were upon economy, efficiency, compliance with law, and strict central control. Both agencies stressed detail, and neither was much concerned during the first decade with public policy or management.

The top leadership of both institutions became distressed, sometimes heatedly, with the Roosevelt New Deal policies. This led in the case of BOB to a complete change in the leadership and in the nature of its work in the 1930s. The leadership of GAO likewise changed in 1939 and again in 1940, but World War II postponed an immediate transformation in its operations until after the war. The Great Depression, the multitude of New Deal programs, and finally World War II made the original routines of budgeting and auditing impracticable if not impossible. Furthermore, there had developed over those years a new and much broadened concept of administration that went well beyond the counting and control of dollars. This view was best set forth in the famous 1937 report of President Roosevelt's Committee on Administrative Management, better known as the "Brownlow report."[8] The Committee envisioned the Bureau of the Budget as the major agent of the president in bringing about better management of the executive branch, and this responsibility was written into BOB's charter in 1939. Later, at the close of World War II, the GAO began moving away from detailed voucher-checking into professional auditing of agency accounts and agency accounting systems. And still later it began what it called "comprehensive auditing" (another misnomer), which encompassed, on a selective basis, financial management generally and even nonfinancial aspects of management.

In the period since about 1950, the parallels between the two agencies, to the extent that they existed at all, are less easy to identify. Both agencies were influenced during the 1950s by the first Hoover commission's call for development of a performance budget with emphasis upon classification of activities, work measurement, and lump-sum appropriations. Both were later influenced by the second Hoover commission and its stress on accrual and cost accounting, and both were affected by the introduction of the so-called planning-programming-budgeting system (PPBS), which was introduced in the Defense Department in 1961 and then extended to the rest of the executive branch in 1965. Ultimately, PPBS probably had more impact upon the GAO than upon BOB/OMB because of the attention it directed to the analysis of policies and programs and their results, which became the main course of GAO's fare during the 1970s. Indeed, this shift in emphasis constituted the second transformation of the GAO.

During all of this 30-year period, the vicissitudes of presidents and Congresses and the relations between them had profound, but quite dissimilar, influences upon the two agencies. Probably the most important legislative event was the Congressional Budget and Impoundment Control Act of 1974. It was one of several manifestations of the resurgence of Congress in national power, which affected the two agencies in divergent ways. It was but one of a number of forces and events that drove the OMB in the direction of political responsiveness to presidential influence. But, if anything, it probably strengthened GAO's resolve to maintain political neutrality.

In the light of the widely different developments of BOB/OMB and GAO in the three decades after 1950, they are here treated in separate chapters [in *A Tale of Two Agencies*]. Chapter 4 deals with BOB/OMB; Chapter 5, with GAO. The closing chapter endeavors to synthesize these two and indeed the earlier parts of the book, to show how the two agencies have related to each other, how they compare and contrast, and how they fit into America's divided scheme of government. Almost the entire book to that point deals with the first 60 years following the effective date of the Budget and Accounting Act of 1921, and most of it concerns the period up to the inauguration of President Reagan in 1981. I have added two epilogues. The first treats the first 15 months of the Reagan budget experience. Rather little can yet be said about the GAO because the new comptroller general, Charles A. Bowsher, did not assume his office until the fall of 1981, shortly before these lines were written. Epilogue II is a brief evocation of the nostalgia of the past and present employees of GAO, BOB, and OMB. In the middle of the book is an Interlude concerning the buildings that have housed the two agencies from their beginnings.

Frederick C. Mosher

NOTES

1. See the Act to Establish the Treasury Department, Public Law 1-12, 2 September 1789.

2. In subsequent pages, BOB and OMB will be referred to by their single names when discussed in their separate time periods. When the organization is treated through time, it will be designated BOB/OMB.

3. For fuller, though still brief, discussion of the literature about both agencies, see the Preface and Acknowledgements of *A Tale of Two Agencies*.

4. Undoubtedly the most prominent example is Elmer B. Staats, who served as deputy director of BOB under four presidents (Truman to Johnson) and then as comptroller general during five presidencies or parts thereof (Johnson to Reagan). Others have included Harry Havens, Philip S. Hughes, and Thomas D. Morris, all of whom held high offices in BOB/OMB and later became assistant comptrollers general in GAO.

5. The Congressional Budget Office (CBO) might offer a similar contrasting posture relative to the OMB, but it is relatively young, and its experience is not yet as rich as that of the GAO.

6. Reorganization Act, Public Law 79-263, 20 December 1945.

7. Such outlays have somewhat misleadingly been described as "uncontrollable" in recent budgets; they are now believed to comprehend three-quarters of the federal budget. But there are degrees of uncontrollability and there are differentials in time. Some items that are not controllable in the current or in the next (budget) year may be controllable in years following. Most federal outlays must be sanctioned in appropriations bills and authorized in separate and prior substantive legislation, much of which precludes any real discretion in the appropriations process. In 1981, the Reagan administration, with the assent of majorities in Congress, showed that some items theretofore considered uncontrollable could in fact be

changed through the reconciliation process. Whether this experience will prove unique remains to be seen.

8. The three-man committee was chaired by Louis Brownlow and also included Charles E. Merriam and Luther H. Gulick.

CHAPTER SEVEN

The Public Service in the Temporary Society[*]

FREDERICK C. MOSHER

This essay is addressed to two related questions:

With respect to the public administrative services in the United States, where are we and where are we going?

and

How can and should we prepare our public services to meet probable future demands in our systems of higher education and public service management?

But there is a question prior to these which requires attention. It concerns the changing nature and probable future directions of the society from which the public services are drawn, within which they operate, and which they are presumed to serve. This essay therefore begins with some observations about the society and its demands upon government, including some of the underlying

---

*Reprinted with permission from Public Administration Review *(January/February 1971)* © *by the American Society for Public Administration (ASPA), 1120 G Street NW, Suite 700, Washington, DC 20005. All rights reserved.*

dilemmas that seem to me most salient to the public service of the near future. Its second part is a discussion of the probable implications of these social directions and dilemmas for public administrative organizations, the public service, public personnel systems, and the universities.

I pretend no expertise in that increasingly popular field of study and speculation known as futuristics. No predictions are offered about the public services and the society of the United States in the year 2000. My ambition is more modest. It is to cull from our experience of the last few years—the decade of the 1960s—some probabilities about the next few—the decade of the 1970s; and to deduce from these what we (in public administration) should be doing about it. The didactic tenor of many of the sentences which follow, the frequent use of the unqualified verb "will," conveys falsely a sense of confidence and even omniscience on the part of the author. All should be qualified by the adverb "probably"; and I would hesitate to give a numerical value to the margins of error. The prognostications are tentative and hopefully provocative, not definitive.

THE SOCIETY AND ITS GOVERNMENTS: THE TEMPORARY SOCIETY

"The Temporary Society" is an expression cribbed from the book of that title by Warren G. Bennis and Philip E. Slater[1] and is used here in two senses, only the second of which is theirs. In the first sense, the society is temporary in that it is widely known and appreciated that it is changing rapidly and will, in effect, be transformed into another society within a relatively short span of years, say 10 or 15. Societies of the past have of course changed, particularly in the West, but none with such speed and few with such awareness. Basic social changes of long ago can, by historians, be described in terms of eras; later, in terms of centuries; more recently in terms of generations. But the "social generation" of today is considerably shorter than the "human generation." The parent of the 1970s is preparing his infant offspring for a society not the same as his own and not even once removed from his own. It is more nearly twice removed.

The second sense in which our society may be described as temporary concerns the institutions and organizations within it and the attachments, the moorings of those individuals who compose it. Bennis, in his chapters of the earlier-cited work, connotes the term with the allegedly changing nature of productive organizations and the evolving patterns of individual roles and associations within them.

> The social structure of organizations of the future will have some unique characteristics. The key word will be "temporary." There will be adaptive, rapidly changing *temporary* systems . . . of diverse specialists, linked together by coordinating and task-evaluating executive specialists in an organic flux—this is the organization form that will gradually replace bureaucracy as we know it.[2]

Although he acknowledges that "the future I describe is not necessarily a 'happy one,'"[3] Bennis is basically optimistic about the prospect as releasing the individual, encouraging his revitalization, and legitimizing fantasy, imagination, and creativity. Slater, in his discussion of the social consequences of temporary systems and particularly of the effects upon the family, is less reassuring.

In both of the senses here described, the term "temporary society" may exaggerate and overdramatize. As any student of anthropology or reader of Arnold Toynbee knows, no society is permanent, although some manage to survive with little change for some centuries. And clearly there are still many stable organizations in the United States and a good many people who do have firm organizational and institutional mooring—probably a solid majority in fact. But in both senses the trend toward temporariness seems likely; and both have significance for the American public service of the future.

OTHER OBSERVATIONS AND ASSUMPTIONS

First among the other assumptions that seem to me most significant for purposes of this discussion is one that is negative, though, from my point of view at least, optimistic: that, in the next several years, there will be no nuclear holocaust, no civil war between races or other groups, no revolution which suddenly overthrows governments or other established institutions, or which reverses existing systems of values and beliefs. In other words, while social change and changes in institutions and behavior will continue with a rapidity at least equal to that of the present, steps in the future will be made from footprints marked today and in the recent past.

A second assumption has to do with the extent the depth, and the application of human knowledge. The era since World War II has been variously labeled: the postindustrial revolution, the scientific revolution, the professional revolution, the information revolution, the cybernetic revolution, the knowledge explosion, the technological era. The emphases among these various pseudonyms have differed, but the central themes are compatible: that knowledge, particularly in the hard sciences and in technology, is growing at a rapid rate, and, as it is applied to the affairs of people, is bringing about rapid and tremendous changes in the nature of society and the capabilities, the values, and the behavior of human beings. Furthermore, in the words of Paul T. David, ". . . the oncoming world of the future, however described, will evidently be a world of increasing potential for human intervention and control both good and bad."[4] As a correlate, knowledge itself, its procreation and its application, have assumed greater and greater importance in the eyes of men, as have the institutions which develop, apply, and transmit it. Wealth, or income-producing ability, is increasingly perceived as knowledge, and its application, decreasingly as property. It is here assumed that this emphasis will continue.

A third assumption concerns the role of government in determining the strategies, the courses and means of action, for the future. Government has ceased to be merely the keeper of the peace, the arbiter of disputes, and the provider of common and mundane services. For better or worse, government has directly and indirectly become a principal innovator, a major determiner of social and economic priorities, the guide as well as the guardian of social values, the capitalist and entrepreneur or subsidizer and guarantor of most new enterprises of great scale. This development has added to American politics and public administration dimensions both of scope and range and of centrality and importance for which the only precedents occurred in the conduct of the World Wars and during the depth of the Great Depression of the 1930s. On virtually every major problem and every major challenge and opportunity we turn to government—whether it be the cultivation of the ocean bottom, control of the weather, exploration of outer space, training the disadvantaged for jobs, providing day-care centers for working mothers, controlling population growth, eliminating discrimination on the basis of race or sex, juggling the interest rate, reducing the impact of schizophrenia, rescuing a bankrupt railroad, safeguarding children from dangerous toys, or cleaning the air. True, government can turn its back on problems, but if the problems continue to fester and grow, it will eventually have to confront them. True, too, government relies heavily upon organizations and individuals in the private sector to carry out many of its programs, but it cannot escape responsibility for guidance, regulation, often financial support, and results.

Finally, the variety and range of governmental responsibilities, coupled with the continuing development of new knowledge and new techniques with which to deal with them, have added enormously to the reliance of the whole society upon the people who man governmental posts, who collectively make its decisions. This is true of officials in all three branches of government, but it is most conspicuous and probably also most significant of the elective and appointive officers in the executive agencies. As the range of public problems and programs broadens, and as knowledge relevant to each grows and deepens, it becomes less and less possible for politically elected representatives to get a handle on more than a few of the significant issues. Even on these, they must rely heavily upon the information, analysis, and judgment of the appointive public servants. This reliance upon administrative personnel will, I assume, continue to grow.

ANOMALIES

There are other areas relevant to the public service of tomorrow where the signals are less clear, where we seem to be moving in two or more directions at once. One of these concerns *rationality* and *objectivity* in reaching public decisions. It is epitomized by the system known as planning-programming-budgeting (PPBS), which future historians may consider the most significant administrative innovation of the 1960s. PPBS in some form and to some degree is now installed in most federal agencies—all the large ones—in the majority of states, and in many of the largest cities and counties. It is doubtful that any definition would satisfy all students and practitioners of PPBS, but most would agree that a central feature is the objective analysis of the probable costs and effectiveness of alternative courses of action to achieve goals, independent of political considerations (in the narrow sense of "political"), bureaucratic considerations, and personal wishes or hunches. In the words of one federal official: "PPBS is simply a means to make public decision making more rational."

Yet, during this same decade of PPBS rationality, there were at least three waves of thought or practice which were distinctively "unrational," if not "antirational." The first was the realist school, which argued that public decisions, particularly budgetary decisions, are incremental in nature, based on last year's experience, seldom responsive to overall, comprehensive analysis. Year-to-year changes are relatively small in amount and reflect estimates of what the political market will bear rather than optimization in allocation of resources. Outcomes are the products of bargaining within fairly narrow ranges of political feasibility. Finally, policy decisions should give at least as much weight to political as to economic costs and benefits.

A second nonrational school of thought of the 1960s is that now widely known as organizational development, an outgrowth of the earlier human relations movement. Its focus is upon the affective rather than the cognitive or analytical aspects of organizational behavior, and its premise is that organizational effectiveness (or health) will be improved if each member understands himself as a personality, is sensitive of the feelings of his associates, and is given a significant discretionary role in the shaping and carrying out of organizational goals. Among its bywords are openness, sensitivity, confrontation, democratic leadership, participation, flat hierarchy (if any at all), organization by objective.

The third movement of the 1960s is more clearly antirational than these other two, at least in the sense that term is used here. It is the politics of confrontation, which must by this time be familiar to most Americans. Its premises are moral categorical imperatives. Certain conditions or actions or decisions are wrong, in the sense not of being incorrect, but of being evil. Such wickedness—whether it be war or racial discrimination or police brutality or alleged repression or the college grading system—is immediately apparent and should be instantly corrected. There is neither need nor time to analyze costs and consequences before taking action against things that are, on their face, evil. It is understandable but paradoxical that the politics of confrontation was born on the campuses of universities that one might have expected would be the seats of rationality and tolerance. But clearly it is a phenomenon of our times that must be reckoned with in the public service. Already, it is being practiced within some governmental agencies and is supported by a growing literature including some writings in the field of public administration.

Though their premises are different, it appears entirely possible that the incremental approach to decision making and the approach of organizational development can be reconciled with the rationality approach of PPBS. In fact, some students and practitioners have argued that policy analysis can be used effectively to enrich, rather than undermine, the bargaining process behind public decisions. There has been less dialogue between the PPBS proponents and the disciples of organizational development. Yet, in one agency, the Department of State, the same group of officers endeavored to introduce both types of approaches at about the same time during the mid-1960s. Neither effort succeeded, but it was the conclusion of many participants that the systems approach failed because organizational development had begun too late. Reconciliation between the rationality emphasis and the politics of confrontation appears less likely because the two are so diametrically opposed in their central premises.

EMPHASES ON SYSTEMS AND PROCESSES

A second area in which the crystal ball seems cloudy concerns the conflicting emphases upon *systems* and *processes*. The charge has been leveled by more than one critic that the study and the practice of government have overemphasized the processes through which decisions are reached and executed with too little consideration of the effects or outcomes of those decisions and actions.[5] They question—I think correctly—the assumption that if the democratic and administrative processes are legal and proper, the consequences will be optimal, or at least the best that is feasible in the American polity. They contest the line of thought growing from Bentley, that given appropriate access to decision channels, interest groups will conflict, balance each other out, and force proper decisions. Finally, they feel that too much faith has been lodged in the procedures governing nominations, elections, interest group access, the merit system, the budget system, and other related processes in the confidence that they will result in the best policies; in short, in a political/administrative "invisible hand" quite comparable to the market system so long relied upon by economists. Manifestly, the "invisible hand" has been less than optimally successful in both the political and economic realms. Yet, while the systems approach, which would analytically seek the best solutions to our public problems, is gaining in both administrative and academic circles, the emphasis upon process continues. In fact, the thrust of behavioralism in political and administrative sciences, with its undertones of determinism, tends to give it added support.

Frederick C. Mosher

PARTICIPATION

The current and increasing popularity of *participation* in decision making and in administration generally is a third source of confusion. It appears in at least three quite different forms. One is participation by those citizens most directly affected by given programs in decisions about those programs and their operations. Epitomized in the Economic Opportunity Act by the expression "maximum feasible participation," variations on the theme are found in a good many other federal programs, and some of them, like the draft, price control, and agricultural allotments, have a long history. It has been prominent at the local level in the drives to return the control of schools to local district boards and to govern the police through citizen review boards. A second manifestation of the participation drive has been the rapid growth of unionism, collective bargaining, and strikes of public servants. A third is the movement, mentioned earlier, toward organizational development, which includes among its central tenets participation, individually and in groups, in decision making.

Participation in decisions affecting public policy by any group of citizens (including employees) not politically representative of the whole or responsible to such political representation may, in theory and sometimes in practice, collide with that central premise of American governance that Redford has described as "overhead democracy."[6] The expression describes a polity resting ultimately on majority control through political representatives, wherein administrative officers are primarily responsible and loyal to their superiors for carrying out the directions of the elective representatives. Of course, legislatures may, and frequently have, delegated to citizen and employee participants policy areas over which they have discretion. But the proper and feasible limits of such delegation remain hazy.

All three types of participation mentioned here offer potential opposition to the ideal of rationality, and all three may lead—and sometimes have led—to the politics of confrontation. Participation by private citizens runs a collision course with the drive toward professionalization, which is discussed later.

DECENTRALIZATION TRENDS

Associated and sometimes identified with the participation thesis is the recent push toward *decentralization* of governmental policy and action to lower levels—from Washington to regional offices or to states, cities, or school districts; from states to local jurisdictions; from cities and counties to community organizations and districts. The paradox is that the decade of the 1960s was one of the most vigorously centralizing eras in our history except in wartime. And there is no sign that the trend is slackening, despite the pleas for decentralization. Growth, technology, population mobility are forcing geographic interdependence; and interdependence forces centralization in public (as well as private) policy. The people of California have a stake in the educational standards of Mississippi, as do those of Buffalo in the waste disposal practices of Cleveland, those of New York in the economic and manpower situation in Puerto Rico, and all of us in the antipollution devices put on new cars in Detroit. The advantage of the federal government and some of the states in access to revenues encourages centralization, as does the failure of many states and local units to realize their own revenue potential in response to public needs.

Continuing centralization seems inevitable; yet decentralization is a plain necessity. Only a small share, in number if not in importance, of public decisions should or can be made in Washington. The federal structure is so functionally specialized as to make broad developmental decisions on a geographic basis extremely difficult—whether for a federal region, a state, a city, or a community. A challenge for administrators of the present and future is to devise, test, effect, and operate mechanisms whereby we can move in both directions at the same time.[7] That is: devices for communities to initiate and make community decisions within regional and/or state guidelines, standards, and policies, and within nationwide objectives and standards. Already there are experiments with such mechanisms, as in the poverty program, model cities, and education. The recent proposal by CED for a two-tier, federated system for metropolitan government with a powerful metropolitan unit and semiautonomous community units is a move in the same two directions.

SPECIALIZATION AND PROFESSIONALIZATION

Another anomaly arises from the narrowing and deepening of *specialization* and *professionalization* among organizations, fields of knowledge, and individuals. This phenomenon, which has been remarked by a great many writers before this one, is particularly significant in governmental enterprises, partly because professionalism has become so prevalent in so many public fields; partly because so many important public organizations are dominated by a single professional elite. As the focus of specialisms has narrowed, the boundaries around social problems have broadened and fuzzed. A consequence is that few professions can now claim total competence to handle basic problems even within those functional areas in which they once were recognized as exclusive monopolists. This is a product of growing *functional interdependence*, which is entirely comparable to the growing geographic interdependence mentioned earlier, and of the external effects—both costs and benefits—of actions taken in one field upon others. It would probably be more accurate to say that the growth has been less in the actual interdependence of different fields and more in the recognition of such interdependence. Crime is no longer a problem for the police alone nor health for doctors alone nor highways for engineers alone nor justice for lawyers alone. Progressive practitioners and educators are articulating and deploring the limitations of their own fields with increasing shrillness. As will be discussed later, this dilemma is bringing about a rethinking of professional—and interprofessional—education and practice.

GROWTH

A final anomaly for our future public administration is the impending desanctification of *growth*, particularly economic growth, as the ultimate goal of society and its rate as the measure of social progress. The process of defrocking has begun. Already it is clear: that overall population growth must ultimately be reduced to zero—and "ultimately" may not be very many decades away; that our largest, "greatest" cities are near-disaster areas for many of their inhabitants; that the biggest organizations are among the most dangerous threats to resources, environment, culture, and even people.

John Kenneth Galbraith, after emphasizing growth as a dominant and pervasive goal of the "technostructure," notes that it is supported by its consistency with the more general goal of economic growth. "No other social goal is more strongly avowed than economic growth. No other test of social success has such nearly unanimous acceptance as the annual increase in the Gross National Product."[8] But faith in GNP growth as an indicator of social betterment must soon decline in the face of its increasingly apparent clumsiness and flimsiness. Expenditures for war and defense are of course part of GNP, and indeed the surest way to increase it rapidly would be a major (nonnuclear) war. The social costs incident to productive enterprise and urbanization are nowhere deducted from GNP: despoliation of resources, pollution of all kinds, crime and other costs related to population density, and many others. Further, whatever dollar expenditures are made to counteract these real costs are *added into*, not *deducted from*, GNP.[9] The costs of producing and merchandising goods that are trivial, worthless, or actually damaging (like tobacco, liquor, guns, and DDT) are part of GNP. And GNP of course takes no account whatever of the distribution of income and wealth among the population.

Of course, much work has already been done toward the development of more sensitive and meaningful measures of social betterment than GNP. The harder and probably slower job will be to modify the underlying faith in growth per se that has served us reasonably well for many decades: the faith that equates "more" with "better" and "growth" with "progress." Administrators cannot much longer rely upon crude measures of growth—whether or not economic—to provide their goals or to appraise their effectiveness. They must help to find, and must learn and apply subtler and more qualitative goals and indices; and they must play some part in communicating these to the public.

To recapitulate: The emerging public administration, the truly "new" public administration, will bear responsibilities of a range and an importance that are hardly suggested in any current textbook. It will have to anticipate and deal with changes in a society that is changing more rapidly than any in human history. It, too, will have to be rapidly changeable and flexible. It will have to press for greater rationality and develop and utilize ever more sophisticated tools for rational decisions, at the same time accommodating to forces that seem unrational. It must concern itself more than in the past with human goals "life, liberty, and the pursuit of happiness"— but without damage to the processes that make democracy viable. And these goals must be more sophisticated than simple quantitative growth. It must recognize the functional and geographic interdependence of all sectors of the society without too much sacrifice to the values of professional specialism and local interest. It must develop collaborative workways whereby centralization and decentralization proceed simultaneously, and assure high competence at every level of government.

These are tall orders for public administration. Their implications are described more specifically in the balance of this article.

IMPLICATIONS FOR PUBLIC ORGANIZATIONS

The statements about public organizations which follow are not purely predictive. All have some basis in observations of current developments. And all are responsive to the societal trends and problems described earlier.

First are the increasing emphasis in and among organizations upon problems and problem solving, and the growing distrust of established and traditional routines, which have failed to provide solutions.

There will be increasing dependence upon, and increasing acceptance of, analytical techniques in planning and evaluating public programs, centering upon specialized units near the top of agencies, but spreading downwards to lower and operating echelons seeking rationalized defenses of their programs. One might anticipate, too, a broadened and more sophisticated approach to analytic techniques that takes into account elements beyond purely economic and quantitative considerations. But there will be increasing concern about long-term objectives, alternative measures for reaching such objectives, social—as distinguished from purely economic—indicators, and improved information systems concerning both costs and effects of programs. There will also be more efforts toward experimentation in undertakings whose prospects are untried and unproven.

As the interconnection and interdependence of social problems is increasingly perceived, there will be growing reliance upon ad hoc problem-solving machinery—task forces, commissions, special staffs to executives, interagency committees, and institutionalized though ad hoc mechanisms within agencies.

Both the second and third developments cited above will force increased attention on the inherently obstinate problems of translating new or changed program decisions into effective action through—or in spite of—existing and traditional agencies and operations. In fact, one of the weakest links in public administration today is that of giving operational meaning to planning decisions, however sophisticated may be the analysis behind the plans and however effective the collaboration in reaching agreement on the plans.

Political executives, under unrelenting pressure from elements in the society and dissatisfied with the answers available from the established bureaucracy, tend to develop and utilize machinery directly responsible to them for developing new programs and changing old ones. At the national level, this is manifest in the emergence of the National Security Council, the new Domestic Council, and a number of presidential program initiatives. Governors like Rockefeller and mayors like Lindsay have responded in substantially comparable ways. So have strong department heads, dissatisfied with recommendations, or lack thereof, from established line bureaus.

There will continue to be vigorous attacks against "entrenched" bureaucracies within departments and agencies. They may be expressed through reorganizing a bureau out of business or scattering its functions or taking over key activities such as planning, personnel, and budget or politicizing its top positions.

Partly in self-defense, bureaus and comparable agencies will undertake to broaden their bases and broaden their capabilities through the engagement of people in relevant specializations but not typical of the elite profession of the bureau. They will also increasingly seek and welcome collaborative relationships with other bureaus and agencies and with other levels of government. And they, too, will become more problem oriented.

As these characteristics of problem orientation and collaboration develop at one level of government, particularly the federal, they will encourage and sometimes enforce comparable approaches at other levels with which it deals.

As local constituencies become more vociferous and more vigorous, and as the capabilities of personnel in federal regional offices, the states, and local governments are upgraded, there will be growing demand for decentralizing decision-making power. My guess is that this kind of decentralization will proceed, but a little more slowly than the centralization process implied above.

Finally, there will be a growing premium on responsiveness to social problems and speed in planning and taking action on them. This will be forced, in part, by the politics of confrontation, mentioned earlier.

In short, administrative organizations will be more political, especially at the leadership levels, in the broader, Aristotelian sense of politics, but not with any loss of brain power and specialized knowledge. The movements toward the latter and the need for them will continue to grow. Agencies, though continuing to reflect a heavy functional emphasis in their structure, will necessarily look beyond their specific functions to related functions and agencies. And they will be more flexible.

These developments will not occur equally in all public agencies any more than they have to date. Indeed, there are a good many public activities for which they will not occur at all. They will be most evident in those problem areas of articulate public concern and in connection with new or radically changed programs; that is, in controversial fields. There will be an abundance of President Truman's "kitchens" around Washington and in other capitals in the United States. One can foresee no diminution of intra and interorganizational conflict.

Partly as a result of the developments suggested above, there will probably be profound changes within administrative organizations in their patterns and behavior styles. The old Weberian description of bureaucracy, with its emphasis upon formal structure, hierarchy, routinization, and efficiency in its narrow sense, is rapidly becoming obsolete in many organizations. It is inadequate particularly for "thought" organizations, agencies that operate within a particularly turbulent political environment, agencies facing increasing complexity in their programs, and agencies staffed heavily with highly professional or scientific personnel. Such organizations must, if they are to survive, be responsive, adaptive, flexible, creative, and innovative. This means, among other things, that they will increasingly be structured around projects or problems to be solved rather than as permanent, impervious hierarchies of offices, divisions, and sections. Permanent hierarchical structures will remain for a variety of administrative purposes and for the affixing of final responsibility. But work itself will be organized more collegially on a team basis. Generalist decisions will be reached through the pooling of the perspectives and techniques of a variety of specialists. Leadership will be increasingly stimulative and collaborative rather than directive.

This "new" style of bureaucracy is not wholly wishful nor simply the paraphrasing of the writings of social psychologists about what an organization ought to be. The movement toward it is evident in many public and private enterprises and dominant in a few, particularly those involved in research and development, such as units of NASA, NIH, and the scientific laboratories. It is more and more prevalent in the social fields, as illustrated by their growing reliance upon intra and interagency task forces, work groups, and committees. It is reflected also in the nature and assignments of a large portion of the so-called political appointees who are not politicians and whose party regularity is incidental, if not, in some instances, totally irrelevant. Many of these appointments appear to be predicated upon professional competence in an appropriate field, ability to apply their skills to a variety of problems, and competence in working with and through (rather than over) others.

IMPLICATIONS FOR THE PUBLIC SERVICE

More than half of the products of the nation's universities and colleges, graduate and undergraduate, are educated in specializations that are intended to prepare them for one or another professional or scientific occupation. Not including housewives, the majority of the other college graduates will later return for professional graduate training or will enter upon some line of work, like the Foreign Service, wherein they will acquire the accoutrements of professionalism on the job. Ours is increasingly a professional society or, more accurately, a professionally led society.

And American governments are principal employers of professionals. Very probably within a few years as many as two-fifths of all professionals in this country will be employed directly or indirectly by governments. I perceive no signals that this trend toward professionalism in government will decline. The programs now developing to help the underprivileged find satisfying careers in government and elsewhere may involve lowering educational requisites for some kinds of jobs. But the extent that such programs are successful will be measured by the numbers of their participants who rise to professional or at least paraprofessional levels. What is challenged is not professionalism but the orthodoxy of the traditional routes to attain it.

Books can and should be written about the impact of professionalism upon the public service. I would like to mention very briefly only a few implications that seem salient to this discussion.

Professionals generally, though not universally, have an orientation to problems or cases; they are prepared to move from one problem to another, somewhat different one, or to keep several balls in the air at the same time. The problem orientation described above in connection with public organizations is entirely in keeping with the professional way of life.

All professions (with the possible exception of the ministry) view themselves as rational, but their ways of viewing and defining rationality vary widely. Rationality is no monopoly of administrators, economists, or lawyers. Probably the nearest approach to pure rationality, with respect to any given problem, must be the product of a mix of differing professional perspectives on that problem.

Professional study and practice has tended to foster increasing specialism and increasing depth, decreasing breadth of both student and practitioner, in the professions. This has been further encouraged by the explosion of knowledge in most fields. Until quite recently it has tended to crowd out the consideration of general social consequences of professional behavior and the philosophical consideration of social values from both education and practice. In most fields it has also minimized education or practice in politics, administration, or organization.

Insofar as professionalism requires many years of training and experience (varying in different fields) in specialized subjects, it has an inhibiting effect upon movement from one occupation to another. But it encourages mobility from place to place and from organization to organization (or self-employment), especially when the move promises new and greater challenges. This is probably truest among the best qualified, most innovative, and most problem-oriented individuals.

Professional behavior tends to be conditioned more by the norms, standards, and workways of the profession than by those that may be imposed by an employing organization. Within those standards professionals seek a considerable degree of autonomy and discretion in the application of their particular skills. They resist working under close supervision of others, especially when the others are not members of the same profession.

When professionals work on problems requiring a number of different occupational skills—and these include almost all problems in the social arena—they prefer to work with others on an equal or team basis, founded in mutual respect.

Frederick C. Mosher

Most of the professions are increasingly grounded in some branches of science. Science is in turn grounded in the search for truth and, for any given problem, the finding of the correct answer. Scientists—and many professionals—are intolerant of ambiguity, of politics, and all too often of other ways of looking at problems.

These alleged attributes of professionalism of course do not apply equally to all professions nor equally to all members of any given profession. Where and to the extent that they do apply, it may be noted that some of them are entirely congruent and encouraging to the kind of organizational behavior suggested in the preceding section. These include:

- orientation to problems, projects, and cases;
- mobility or willingness to move from place to place and from job to job;
- collegial relationships in working with others on common problems.

But in certain other respects, the education and practice of typical professions is a good deal less than optimal for the public service of tomorrow. First, there is insufficient stress upon and concern about human and social values. All professions allege their dedication to the service of society, and most take for granted that activities their members perform within professional standards are useful and beneficial to the public. There has been rather little reexamination of these assumptions in the face of a rapidly changing society and rapidly expanding governmental responsibilities. And individual practitioners are provided little motivation or intellectual grounding to stimulate concern about general social values in relation to their day-to-day problems. This is only incidentally a matter of codes of ethics, most of which are essentially negative and very few of which even mention any special ethical problems arising from public service, even when substantial portions of the profession are employed by governments. The kind of need I perceive is more of the order, for example, that:

- engineers who plan highways or airports or sewage plants take into consideration the secondary and tertiary effects

of these undertakings on the quality of life in America and in the places for which they are planning;
- lawyers look beyond due process, *stare decisis*, the adversary system, etc., to the roots of our social difficulties;
- economists look beyond primary and quantitative costs and benefits, the market analogy, and the GNP growth rate to where we as a society and as individuals are going—both as a whole and in relation to individual economic decisions; etc.

Second and closely related to the values question is the need of a great many more professionals who have a sophisticated understanding of social, economic, and political elements and problems of our times, including an understanding of the relation of their own work to that setting.

Third is the need for humility and for tolerance of others, their ideas and perspectives, whether or not professionals; and an ability to communicate with others on shared problems.

Fourth is an ability to work in situations that are uncertain and on problems for which there is no correct solution—in short, a tolerance for ambiguity.

Fifth is an understanding of organizations and how they work, particularly in the context of American politics and government; skill in managing in the larger sense of getting things done with and through other people.

Sixth, there should be greater incentive for—and much less discouragement of—creativity, experimentation, innovation, and initiative.

Seventh is the need for a much higher degree of mobility—within agencies, between agencies, between governments, and in and out of government. Despite the observation made earlier that professionalism encourages such mobility, public employment by and large has inhibited it, even for its professionals. One result is that the majority of those who rise to the near top have had effective experience in only one agency, often only one division of that agency. This is a disservice to the man—the absence of challenge and of different and broadening kinds of experiences. It is a misfortune for the government because it tends to solidify bureaucratic parochialism and, in some degree, discourages the problem approach that was stressed earlier. Ten years of experience in one job may be merely one year of experience repeated ten times. The idea of temporariness should extend much further than it has in the civil services of governments.

Finally, there should be greater opportunities for challenge and for rapid advancement for the able young, for the underprivileged, and for women. In government, this means opportunities for professionalizing the nonprofessionals and for rapid advancement through a variety of challenging assignments for those who prove effective.

IMPLICATIONS FOR PERSONNEL SYSTEMS

Obviously, the strengths and weaknesses of the public service can be attributed only partially to personnel systems—the systems whereby people are employed and deployed, advanced, and retired. And changes in the systems have only a partial and usually rather slow influence in changing the nature and calibre of the public service. Yet I doubt that there is any other manipulable element with as much potential impact. The system and its popular image condition the kinds and capabilities of people who seek entrance and their expectations. It also influences the expectations of those already on the job, their motivation, the rewards and penalties of differing kinds of behavior, their movement from job to job, and the way they work together.

Personnel administration has since World War II, but particularly in the decade of the 1960s, been undergoing a radical transition in the national government and, in varying degrees, in the states and the cities. It has been marked by:

- decentralization and delegation from central civil service agencies in the direction of line managers;
- growing emphasis upon personnel as a management service rather than as a control or police activity;

- growth of employee and executive development programs, particularly through institutionalized training;
- growth and recognition of employee organizations and collective bargaining;
- concern about and programs for equal opportunity for the handicapped, underprivileged, minority groups, and women;
- relaxation of rules and requirements for standardized personnel actions, particularly as they apply to professionals;
- "positive" recruitment in the educational institutions and elsewhere.

The extent and significance of these and other changes are not, I think, sufficiently appreciated. If one were to compare an annual report of the U.S. Civil Service Commission of a pre-War year such as 1939 or even of 1955 with *Blueprint for the Seventies*, its report for 1969, he could hardly believe that they were produced by the same agency. (Though a glance at the appendices might make the identity of the three more recognizable.) Most of these changes have been consonant with the changing nature and needs of the society.

Yet there linger some tenets of civil service administration—and the image of them perceived by both bureaucrats and the general public—which seem inconsistent with the directions of the society and dysfunctional in terms of its demands upon the public service. I should like to focus upon two of them, both born of reform movements and both with a distinguished history of about half a century or longer. The first is here referred to as *careerism*. It is that feature built upon the expectation that individuals will be recruited soon after completion of their education; that they will spend the bulk of their working lives in the same organization; that they will be advanced periodically as they gain experience and seniority, such advancement made on the basis of competition with their peers; and that they will be protected in such advancement against competition with outsiders. The second is *position classification*, or, more particularly, the thesis that the content of a given position or class of positions be the hub around which other personnel actions and indeed management generally should revolve.

Careerism has historically been associated with such commissioned corps systems as the Army, Navy, and Foreign Service, but it is now clear that it is equally or more virile in many of the well-established agencies under civil service in the federal and all other levels of government. Typically in the United States—and most other industrialized nations of the world—careers are associated with individual agencies—departments, bureaus, services, divisions—rather than with the government as a whole. And typically they are identified with a particular type of professional specialization, dominant or subordinate, within the given agency. Careerism may contribute to managerial flexibility in the provision of a corps of qualified people within the organization who are available for different kinds of assignments. At the same time, it inhibits overall elasticity in terms of quick changes in total manpower resources or the provision of persons with different kinds of skill and perspectives. It discourages lateral entry or the ingestion of new blood above the bottom or entering level, and some agencies have absolutely banned it. More often than not, careerism provides built-in, though usually unwritten, incentives for individuals to pursue orthodox careers within the agency and to avoid unusual assignments that might sidetrack or delay advancement. Overall, careerism probably is an important discourager of creativity, innovation, and risk taking because of the perceived or imagined dangers of stepping out of line. And insofar as it assures that the older officers within the system will hold the top positions of the agency, it assures continuity, stability, and conservatism in agency policy.[10] It is probably the principal ingredient of the cement that binds an agency into a strong, autonomous, and perhaps impervious entity against outsiders—whether above in the Executive Branch or outside in the legislature or the public.

It is apparent that many aspects of careerism run counter to effective government responsiveness to the needs of the temporary society. Among the items it discourages are: collaborative relationships with other agencies and specializations toward the solution of common problems; interchange of personnel among agencies, among jurisdictions of government, and between government and the private sector; ad hoc but temporary assignments that are unorthodox in terms of career advancement; responsiveness and rapid change to meet rapidly changing problems. Insofar as the gates of entry upon a government career are based upon orthodox educational credentials—and most of them are—it inhibits employment programs for aspiring potential professionals of minority groups. The bar against lateral entry effectively shuts out mature and qualified women after they have raised their families. And the whole image of government as life-long career systems in single agencies discourages some of the most alert, idealistic, and action-oriented of American youth.

Like careerism, position classification is not necessarily a dysfunctional process. Indeed, it is hard to imagine any sizable organization operating without at least a skeleton of a classification plan, even if it is unwritten. The problem arises from the centrality and dominance that positions and their classification came to assume in personnel administration, in management generally, and in the psychology of officers and employees. Thirty years ago classification had become the jumping-off point for most activities in the field of personnel: pay, recruitment and selection, placement, promotions, transfers, efficiency ratings, even training. It provided the blocks for what some have called the building-block theory of organization—an essentially static and mechanistic concept. It was the restraining leash around the necks of aggressive public managers, and the more successful of them were often the ones who could successfully slip or unfasten it. It has subtler though perhaps more important negative effects upon such matters as status, motivation, willingness to work with others on common problems, communications, flexibility, and adaptability: in short, pervasive impairment to what Agyris has labeled "organizational health."

The whole concept of position classification runs somewhat counter, or restraining, to the concept of organization as a fluid, adaptive, rapidly changing entity, oriented to problems and motivated by organizational objectives. To the extent that it is coercive and binding, detailed and specific, and difficult to change, classification has the effects of:

— retarding organizational change and adaptation;

- discouraging initiative and imagination beyond the definition of the position class;
- inhibiting special, ad hoc assignments or otherwise working "out of class";
- discouraging recognition of unusual contributions and competence through rapid advancement.

Bennis confidently predicted that: "People will be differentiated not vertically according to rank and role but flexibly according to skill and professional training."[11] His forecast is not totally reassuring, since "skill and professional training" sound suspiciously like credentialism, and differentiation by credentials can certainly be vertical. But it is clear that the dominance of classification in government has declined a great deal and nearly vanished in some sectors except as a convenience to management. In the federal government the flexibility of the management intern and FSEE programs at the lower rungs of the ladder and, to a slight degree, of the Executive Manpower System at the upper rungs are examples. But clearly in many federal agencies and state and local governments we need to go much further and faster.[12]

I have not intended in this section to suggest that governments cease assuring careers to prospective and incumbent employees, nor that position classification be abandoned. Both seem to me essential. But some of the unintended consequences of both could and should be alleviated in terms consonant with the trends of the society and its demands on government. What is really needed is a PPBS-type analysis of public personnel practices in terms of their long-range costs and benefits toward governmental objectives. My prediction is that such analyses would indicate that there should be:

- a deemphasis of careerism and tenurism;
- more lateral entry, exit, and reentry;
- more mobility and flexibility in assignment and reassignments;
- rewards rather than implicit penalties for broadening experience in other agencies, other governments, and the private sector;

- more emphasis in rank, status, and rewards upon the man and his performance, less upon his position description;
- declining reliance upon examinations and rank-order lists in entrance and advancement, and more reliance upon performance and references;
- more opportunities for reeducation and retraining, and for broadening education and training, especially for professional personnel;
- more emphasis upon rewards and recognition for initiative and work well done, with less concern about discipline and penalties for nonconformity;
- broadening of the subjects of negotiation in collective bargaining and, with some exceptions, recognition of the right to strike.

IMPLICATIONS FOR THE UNIVERSITIES

The proper mission and role of higher education in American society is today more in dispute than ever before. I acknowledge my bias in thinking that the universities and colleges do and should have a broad responsibility for preparing public leaders for their occupational roles. But this is not to be construed, as it has been in many places and many fields in the past, as a narrowly vocational preparation. In the majority of professions it is increasingly recognized that most techniques and workways of day-to-day operations are best learned on the job. But the universities are uniquely qualified to provide a theoretical base and some methodological principles for such techniques. They are also equipped to open the students' minds to the broader value questions of the society and of their professions' roles in that society. As the procreators and warehouses of knowledge in vast ranges of fields, they can provide some comprehension of social and political complexity, and of the interconnection and interdependence of social problems with which they will deal.

The universities have not been as successful in these capacities as they might be. One reason, I think, lies in the history of professional education. The Morrill Act of more than a century ago and the land-grant colleges to which it gave rise were tremendously effective in revolutionizing the technology of agriculture and industry. But they provided what is today an unfortunate heritage that persons can qualify to operate as full-grade professionals with degrees as bachelors, masters, even doctors in their fields with virtually no education beyond that perceived as immediately relevant and necessary to the practice of their profession, plus some grounding in the sciences regarded as foundational to that practice. As some professional education developed in many other fields— education, business administration, forestry, journalism, etc.—a similar pattern was adopted. Later, advances in knowledge tended to drive out or inhibit the development of liberal arts courses in the preparation for some other professions such as medicine and the sciences, physical and social. A majority of our public and private leaders are products of such professional and scientific education, and a good many of them have little systematic study beyond the high school level about the society and culture in which they will live and practice their trades.

This deficiency has been recognized in some universities, in a growing number of professional schools, and in some of the professions themselves. They are seeking to build up offerings and requirements in the humanities and the social sciences. My own feeling is that our minimal target should be that all who go to college should have the equivalent of at least two years of liberal arts beyond the field of their major, and that all aspiring professionals have at least one course that relates their specific profession to the society and to the social problems to which it is relevant. This course should go well beyond the Boy Scout code level of traditional courses in professional ethics.

A second shortcoming of higher education is an outgrowth of the increasing depth and specialization of disciplines and subdisciplines that have been a consequence of the knowledge explosion. These have tended to inhibit interdisciplinary and interprofessional study and to deemphasize the connections and interdependencies that have been stressed earlier in this essay. Recognition of this difficulty is attested by the growth on many campuses of cross-disciplinary institutes that are focused on problem areas rather than the traditional disciplinary divisions. It has also given rise to a growing variety of cross-disciplinary educational programs such as comprehensive health planning, urbanology, city planning and public administration, engineering and medicine, economics and about every professional field, and many others. Such programs should be encouraged, as should the recognition by all college faculties that no discipline is equipped to handle adequately even its own problems by itself.

A third shortcoming of the universities lies in their almost systematic ignoring, if not derogation, of the possibilities of social invention, experimentation, innovation, and direction to resolve and correct public problems; and of the mechanisms whereby these actions can be carried out. This I think is true not alone of most professional schools but also of the humanities and the social and natural sciences, not excluding political science. The academic manifestations of the politics of confrontation are, in some part, a product of frustration; and the frustration is, in some part, a product of ignorance about the potentialities and the tactics of social change in a democratic polity. If the assumptions stated earlier in this article are near the mark, change and innovation are increasingly controllable by human beings, acting through political and administrative mechanisms of government; and they are heavily dependent upon the effectiveness of appointive public administrators who are, in major proportion, products of the universities. To the extent that these institutions fail to arouse interest in and awareness about the challenges, the obstacles, and the mechanics of government and, perhaps worse, to the extent they excite hostility toward politics and public administration, they may in fact be inhibiting the possibilities of real social reform. Recent evidence on many campuses of renewed interest of many professors and students in current problems and in politics may signal a turn in the pendulum: But clearly there is a long way to go.

A fourth area in which the institutions of higher education need accelerated development is continuing education, particularly for those in middle and upper levels of public service. With the rapid growth of knowledge and equally rapid changes in social problems, renewed education for persons already in professional practice has come to be regarded as essential in some fields. There has been some recognition and provision for it in some branches of the public service, but altogether too little. Continuing or mid-career education for public servants of five different types is needed:

1. Refresher or updating education in one's own professional field;
2. Broadening education about social problems and developments—both those directly relevant to the program of one's agency and those widely significant to the continuing understanding of a dynamic society;
3. Education about American politics and government and about public organization and management, especially for those without previous study in these fields who are about to assume responsible administrative positions;
4. Education about newly developed techniques of analysis, data processing, etc., with particular emphasis upon their uses, potential, and limitations;
5. Training in sensitivity, in self-understanding, and in interpersonnel communication, understanding, and adaptation.

For the many reasons cited earlier in this article, programs in all these categories are likely to become increasingly crucial in the years ahead.

A CLOSING NOTE: THE SCHOOLS OF PUBLIC AFFAIRS

During the 1960s there was a considerable growth of new schools in the public affairs area and a substantial redirection of the programs of some of the older ones. Most of these additions and changes have been responsive to the wave of popularity of PPBS and have focused upon techniques of rational analysis of public problems. Within limits, this is a desirable development. Public administration programs of the past were, like governments themselves, not conspicuously strong in hardheaded, sophisticated analysis. Administrators need to know the how's and why's of policy analysis as well as its uses and limitations. But analysis is a tool of decision reaching, not decision making itself; and a solid command of analytical techniques is no assurance of a good administrator. I think it at least as important today as in the heyday of scientific management that we not permit administration, in its response to major public issues, to be mistaken for sophisticated, academically aesthetic techniques.

Yet I feel strongly that schools of public affairs of the future may play a unique and a crucially important role in the improvement of governmental responses to rapidly changing public demands. They will not be a resurrection of the earlier efforts to create a profession built around POSDCORB, nor of current efforts to create a management science based either on sociological theory of organizations or on operations research and PPBS—although all of these will play a part. They will be grounded rather in an understanding of social values, social and governmental institutions, and the mechanisms of induced social and political change; in a sensitivity to the feelings and desires of others, both as groups and individuals and the capacity to reason and work with them in finding and effectuating solutions to problems. They will be motivated by an unremitting search for that elusive but holy ghost, the public interest. They will rely upon the study of problems and the application to those problems of varieties of research techniques, methodologies, and disciplinary and professional perspectives. And this will involve working through and around the multifold obstacles and roadblocks of other human beings generally and governmental institutions particularly.

All of these things obviously cannot be taught on a campus by a single school—or even by all schools and departments severally. The unique role of a school of public affairs is that it can provide a focus on a university campus for those students—both preservice and mid-career—who will spend a significant portion of their working lives in pursuit of public purposes. Many, even most, of its resources will be formally or informally derived from the faculties of other professional schools and other disciplines. And the primary, or at least the initial, major field of the majority of its

Frederick C. Mosher

students will be in studies other than public affairs, broadly defined. It can, and hopefully will, become the central link between governments and the many semiautonomous elements that collectively comprise the multiversity. Its primary and its unique feature is explicit in the first word of its title: *public*.

NOTES

1. Warren G. Bennis and Philip E. Slater, *The Temporary Society* (New York: Harper and Row, 1968).

2. *Ibid.*, 73–74, 76.

3. *Ibid.*, 75.

4. Paul T. David, "The Study of the Future," *Public Administration Review*, Vol. XXVIII, No. 2 (March/April 1968), 193.

5. Among the most forceful of these critics have been Theodore S. Lowi in his book, *The End of Liberalism: Ideology, Policy and the Crisis of Public Authority* (New York: W. W. Norton & Co., 1969), and Allen Schick in his article, "Systems Politics and Systems Budgeting," *Public Administration Review*, Vol. XXIX, No. 2 (March/April 1969), 137–151. Comparable points of view are implicit or explicit in much of the writing of those who are identified with the "new left" in the fields of political science, public administration, other social sciences, and indeed intellectuals in general.

6. Emmette Redford, *Democracy in the Administrative State* (Fairlawn, N.J.: Oxford University Press, 1969), 70.

7. John W. Gardner, whose experience as head of the Department of Health, Education, and Welfare and then of the Urban Coalition would seem to qualify him uniquely on this subject, recently stated the problem succinctly: "I do not believe that major institutional change will be initiated at the local level. Local groups can do a lot of important things—significant, useful things. . . . If you want effective social change, you've got to know what's bothering people and you've

got to have leadership at the local level. But grass-roots leadership without national links just becomes sentimental." Quoted by the Associated Press in *The Daily Progress*, Charlottesville, Virginia, 2 August 1970, 3-A.

8. John Kenneth Galbraith, *The Industrial State* (Boston: Houghton Mifflin, 1967), 173.

9. For a devastating and frightening analysis along this line, see the work by an unusual economist, Ezra J. Mishan, *The Cost of Economic Growth* (New York: Frederick A. Praeger, 1967).

10. Some of the dysfunctional effects of careerism in the upper levels of the U.S. civil service provoked the recent proposal of the Bureau of Executive Manpower, U.S. Civil Service Commission, for changes in the management of super grades. Among many other things, it recommended that super-grade employees be engaged on contracts of five-year duration. Upon completion of the contracts, they could be separated or returned to grade 15 levels or have their contracts renewed on a one-year basis.

11. Bennis and Slater, *op. cit.*, 74.

12. It is noteworthy that a congressional committee recently asked the U.S. Civil Service Commission to conduct a thorough two-year study, now under way, of federal classification and its effects.

CHAPTER EIGHT

A Personal Appreciation: Frederick C. Mosher: Theorist and Practitioner

KENNETH W. THOMPSON

Fritz Mosher was many things, but he was never a bore. Once he was lecturing before a consciousness-raising group at the Federal Executive Institute. They explained that they had to delay his lecture while they sought to interact with one another and explore where they had been in their careers and their goals for their remaining years. In particular they wanted to probe one another's innermost thoughts and their deepest hopes for the future. They asked Fritz the leading question about what he was thinking, and he replied: "I'm thinking how I can give my *?x!!* [expletives deleted] lecture and get out of here so I can get my hair cut."

When he joined the Miller Center he had many requests that were any director's nightmare. He asked if the Miller Center could join in buying an apartment in Washington where he or any Miller Center scholar could stay overnight when they were attending a conference or doing research. It was a perfectly reasonable idea from his standpoint but impossible from mine. Next, he wanted to retain a chaired appointment at the Center but work half-time. I patiently told him that the vice president of finance had told me that no one could be appointed to a chair unless he (she) was on a full-time appointment. Fritz's half-time turned out to be at least time and a half. We finally worked it out, but it took the genius of a U.Va. vice president. Fritz attended conferences and advisory committees. I had been instructed to say that we could pay only if they were specifically a part of Foundation business. Fritz saw such problems as largely the result of stuffy bureaucracy. Most of our conversations were calm and reasoned. A few boiled over into a mild form of congressional debate, but Fritz's anger never lasted long. It was gone almost immediately, like a summer's storm. I also had secretaries to deal with because Fritz wrote more than anyone at the Center and he sometimes tried to persuade secretaries to take on extra work. That at least was their complaint. Fritz also prepared an anthology and was shocked at the permission charges. So was I, but I could think of nothing the Center could do to reduce his burden. He was fed up with me far more often than I was with him. I knew even when he complained that I was in the presence of a giant figure in American political science.

Fritz also brought a hilarious sense of humor to the Center that was contagious. He had the ability to laugh at himself, at me, and at various situations, including ones that were filled with tragic elements. Edith Mosher was hit by a bus in Indonesia, and after the worst was over and they returned to Charlottesville, Fritz couldn't restrain himself from regaling us with the story of medical treatment Indonesian-style. Another part of his story dealt with the airlines. He negotiated with them to provide some form of comfort for Edith for the long flight back to the United States. Finally, they put Edith in first class and Fritz in economy with permission to visit her from time to time. We told him her treatment reflected the fact that she was the better scholar (in fact she is an award-winning scholar on education and politics/administration). By the time he had finished his account of their adventure and the perils of Pauline, we were stretched out in laughter. With a twinkle in his eyes, he would regularly recount such incongruous experiences, but to record them all would require a separate volume.

He was all in favor of our bringing scholars and community together in our Forums. At least that was true in theory. He refused to relax his high standards, however, even when donors were involved. One very generous person in the community became intensely interested in the subject of presidential transitions, a subject on which Fritz was a preeminent authority. Once he gave a late afternoon Forum in the Dome Room of the Rotunda. After the Forum, the particularly generous member of the community came forward and asked Fritz a question. Fritz responded: "That is a stupid question." It took ten years to regain friendly relations with the donor.

Working with younger scholars, he was superb. He gained their lasting affection and respect. Sometimes he met them at the Center, but other times at his home. They had lunch together. They never failed to keep an appointment, perhaps because working with Fritz was an utterly enjoyable experience. He taught them how to organize a book and decide on a research agenda. When their field was other than public administration, he conducted a seminar over coffee or lunch. The *Transition* book evolved in that way. Two absolutely remarkable young graduate students, even after receiving Ph.D.'s, announced with a smile, "We have to get together with Mosher." They did the case studies for the book, but he worked with them in choosing the studies. He had a few disappointments with students, but he staunchly defended them until it was clear they were not going to finish their assignments.

Whether in dialogue with senior colleagues in trying to think through the choice of a new national commission or fill in gaps in knowledge about government and politics, Fritz Mosher was a wellspring of knowledge. He had an encyclopedic mind. When he didn't have answers at hand, he looked them up. I can't remember a single question he couldn't answer. Whenever the consensus was that we would have nothing to contribute on a proposed commission subject, Fritz would show how we might have something to say. I learned there was nothing one couldn't discuss with Fritz, including credible gossip. As he looked out on the world, he expected human frailty, including his own. He was pleased when efforts went well and not surprised when they didn't. As we sat around the table in our early Forums in an increasingly crowded room, Fritz had answers on issues of governance that no one else could provide. He had forgotten more about government and politics that all of us taken together would ever know.

Above all, he taught us how to build loyalty to an institution. He and Edith gave generously to the Miller Center. Giving may have been an ethic he learned from his father, a founder of the Maxwell School of Government at Syracuse. We all remember his attending our Conversations at Monticello when he and Edith had to lean on one another as they trudged up a long walkway from the parking lot. Again, the Moshers asked the tough questions. He was astounding. Until his last breath he never stopped thinking, teaching, and enriching our lives. The legacy of Frederick C. Mosher will always be one of the richest veins to be tapped in the history of the Miller Center.

I.

POLICY: PRINCIPLES, PROCESS, AND PRACTICE

Professor Paul T. David

CHAPTER NINE

Paul Theodore David: In Memoriam

LAURIN HENRY

Paul T. David, Professor Emeritus of Government and Foreign Affairs at the University of Virginia, died of cancer on 7 September 1994 at his home in Charlottesville. Born 12 August 1906 in Brockton, Massachusetts, son of a Methodist minister in a family strongly committed to education and service, he spent most of his youth on the ancestral farm at Onarga, Illinois, where he attended public schools. He graduated from Antioch College in 1928 and from Brown University in 1933 with a Ph.D. in economics. His dissertation, written with the aid of a Brookings Institution fellowship and later published by Brookings, was *The Economics of Air Mail Transportation*.

Paul's professional life was notable both for the variety of institutions in which he worked and the diversity of subjects to which he made influential contributions. He was energetic, a quick study, and always receptive to new challenges. A fortuitous sequence of career moves took him from government service, to professional associations and think tanks, to university teaching and research; from economics, to public policy, to political science, and finally, to very broad social science.

In his first career as a governmental economist, Paul participated in memorable events of the early New Deal. He worked briefly for a congressional committee, and then in 1933 through Antioch president Arthur E. Morgan, who had just been named chairman of the Tennessee Valley Authority, he became, literally, the first employee of TVA. He organized the staging office in Washington, and later in Knoxville; on the economic and social analysis staff during TVA's most creative period, he did odd jobs for Morgan. On the side, somewhat to his own surprise and the consternation of his superiors, he found himself organizing the TVA staff in a white-collar union. At TVA, he had met another protean figure, Floyd W. Reeves of the University of Chicago, and in 1936, when Reeves was tapped for the research on personnel for FDR's Committee on Administrative Management (Brownlow Committee), Paul became his deputy and co-author of a report, *Personnel Administration in the Federal Service*, whose recommendations set the reform agenda on its subject for decades to come. Back in Washington, again with Reeves, he became head of staff and produced a major report for a presidential advisory committee on education. When that group was followed up by the American Council on Education's Commission on Youth, Paul became the associate director and author of a series of important reports on education and youth employment, from depression crisis to postwar planning.

In 1942, Paul reentered government service on the economics staff of the Bureau of the Budget. His assignments were varied, but his economics background and dissertation subject led to his becoming the staff specialist on civil aviation policy for the Bureau and the White House. He was involved in planning and then served as a principal secretariat officer for the 1944 international conference at Chicago to plan a postwar regime in aviation. Following that interest, he transferred to the Department of State, and when the International Civil Aviation Organization (ICAO) was established in Montreal, he was appointed by the President as deputy head of the U.S. delegation, where he served from 1947 to 1950.

By then, Paul's interests were shifting from economics to politics. He had come to think that the critical problems of government arose not so much from technical difficulties of policy and its administration as from underlying political institutions seemingly incapable of offering clear alternatives and mustering majorities coherent enough to give sustained support to reasonable policy choices. In that concern, he joined a group that became the American Political Science Association's Committee on Political Parties; its recommendations, *Toward a More Responsible Two-Party System* (1950), touched off debate in political science about the ideal and actual nature of political parties that continues to this day. For Paul, healthy party competition and its links to policy-making became a recurring theme of research and writing for the remainder of his career.

In 1950, Paul left the government and returned to Brookings. His first major assignment was to direct a study of *Administration of Foreign Affairs and Overseas Operations* (1951)—a project that, if it did not permanently solve the problem, clearly defined the alternatives between which successive administrations fluctuated for many years. Next getting into serious political science, he organized a complex joint project of Brookings and APSA to study the presidential nominations in 1952, from grass-roots caucuses and primaries through the national party conventions. The outcome was a five-volume publication, *Presidential Nominating Politics in 1952* (1954) by David, Malcolm Moos, and Ralph M. Goldman, plus 70 collaborators from academia who provided data from their respective states. This publication was followed by another major study, *The Politics of National Party Conventions* (1960), by David, Goldman, and R. C. Bain. Those two studies made Paul the leading scholarly expert on party governance, nominating processes, and conventions during the ensuing period of rapid reforms in those institutions; he was a frequent adviser to party activists and a commentator in the press. In this time at Brookings he also served as director of governmental studies (1955 to 1958), launching a comprehensive program to complement his own research. In the interstices, he produced other reports and served as co-author and/or editor of less ambitious books such as *Executives for Government* (with Ross Pollock, 1957), and *The Presidential Election and Transition, 1960-61* (with several co-authors, 1961).

After a year at the Center for Advanced Study in the Behavioral Sciences at Stanford, Paul left government and the non-profits in 1960 to join the faculty of the University of Virginia. His teaching area was American politics, particularly parties, elections, and the presidency. In research, he went straight to a critical issue of the time by undertaking, with Ralph Eisenberg, what started as a modest study but bloomed into a major project that produced for every U.S. county a statistical measure of the distortion of representation caused by the apportionment of state legislatures, then still largely unreformed prior to *Baker v. Carr*. *Devaluation of the Urban and Suburban Vote* (1961, 1962) clinched the case for reapportionment and became a handbook for attorneys and reformers as the "One Person-One Vote" principle was implemented throughout the nation in the next few years. Paul later called it his most consequential single piece of work.

In the middle 1960s, Paul served a term as chairman at Virginia, leading the department through a period of rapid expansion of graduate studies, updating of curriculum, and growth of faculty—a modernization required by the institutional situation but not much appreciated by senior colleagues unaccustomed to Paul's straight-ahead style of administration. Also in this period came Paul's most ambitious intellectual endeavor, which was an experimental doctoral program built around a double-credit course that he developed on Processes of Change—all kinds of change, including their origins, patterns, consequences, and what mankind might do to guide them. This course required reading and integration of materials from not only all of the conventional social scientists but the interdisciplinary meta-thinkers as well. After he wrote a few articles about the experiment, Paul discovered that he was considered a futurist. Although students who survived the course called it a fantastic experience, the venture eventually had to be abandoned: the reading list was daunting to most students; Paul found it an almost full-time job to keep the syllabus updated with the proliferating relevant literature; the grant funds and fellowships that had lured students into the program ran out; and other graduate students—and faculty—could not see how this material fitted into the subfields of political science required for the Ph.D. exams. Processes of Change was a success in the context of adult general education, but it could not survive in an environment preoccupied with disciplinary specialization.

Laurin Henry

Paul returned to more conventional political science teaching, but his research continued to have innovative thrusts. A 1967 article on the vice presidency called early attention to possibilities for invigorating that office, and a 1971 piece on "Party Platforms As National Plans" echoed his interest in connecting parties and policy and attracted considerable attention as a novel way of thinking about a generally despised institution. His last major research was a historical analysis of *Party Strength in the U.S., 1872-1970* (1972) based on a measure of party competition he devised. Subsequent articles updated the application of what has become known as "David's Index of Party Strength," and the series is being continued by the Inter-University Consortium on Political and Social Research at the University of Michigan.

After his official retirement in 1977, Paul continued to produce occasional articles on party competition, nominating procedures, and revisiting the "responsible parties" controversy. He traveled widely, both for pleasure and to serve as visiting professor or lecturer at several institutions in the United States and abroad. He was an occasional seminar leader at the Federal Executive Institute and an active participant and adviser at the Miller Center of Public Affairs at the University of Virginia in Charlottesville. A life member of the American Political Science Association (APSA), he submitted to lengthy interviews for the association's Oral History project and painstakingly corrected and extended the transcripts.

Toward the end of his life, Paul was delighted to discover that his early work in international civil aviation was of interest to historians of that subject. His last publication, which was published just before he died, was a detailed memoir of the 1944 Chicago conference, with emphasis on the role of the secretariat, for a volume commemorating the 50th anniversary of the conference in the *Annals of Air and Space Law*. Considering his years and declining health, it was a remarkable feat of clear writing, precise recollection, new reading, and rummaging through archives. He would miss by a few months honors due to be rendered at international conferences celebrating the 50th anniversary of the Chicago conference and the founding of ICAO.

Paul is survived by his wife Opal, a fellow Antiochian whom he met and married in his TVA days, a major force with many accomplishments in public administration, education for women, and local government in Albemarle County. They had no children, but a host of friends and admirers of the achievements of a remarkable team.

CHAPTER TEN

Is it Possible to Move Toward More Responsible Political Parties?*

PAUL T. DAVID

In the late 1940s, Professor David was a member of a Committee on Political Parties established by the American Political Science Association. The Committee's report, whose substantive thrust is suggested by the title Toward A More Responsible Two-Party System *(1950), became and remains controversial, expressing what has generally been a minority viewpoint in the profession. In a 1979 paper, David revisited the Committee experience and the issues it generated. He gave an insider account of how the committee was created and the processes that resulted in its report. He defended the report, arguing that critics had tended to minimize the problems of government to which the report was addressed and overlooked its moderate and carefully qualified statements while attributing extreme views that the Committee did not actually hold. Then he looked again at the possibility and desirability of moving toward more responsible parties in light of the recent party reform experience.*

* * * * *

Is it desirable to move toward a system of more responsible political parties? If it would be desirable, is it possible?

---

*An unpublished paper written in 1979.

Is It Possible to Move Toward More Responsible Political Parties?

Recently it has become increasingly obvious that the influence of the single-issue pressure groups is on the rise. They are, of course, one of the oldest features of American political life, but recently they have multiplied in numbers, financial power, and their ability to intimidate the individual member of Congress.[1] With the parties as weak as they are, the pressure groups no longer feel compelled to work through the parties; the individual member finds himself or herself defenseless. To protect themselves, the members of like-minded groups in Congress need to band together. If the parties were performing their historic functions, the banding together might most easily take place through the medium of the two political parties. Probably most professional students of government agree that this path would be desirable.

In these days of party weakness, it may seem impossible to move the parties toward more internal strength and capacity for responsibility. Yet the case needs a fresh examination in the light of the institutional and other changes of recent years. The parties and the party system have continued to evolve since 1950. That evolution has been the product of forces so massive and so diffused that they almost defy analysis. Students of the party system are in reasonable agreement on what has happened but are far from agreement on any precise analysis of the causes, which leaves the field wide open for speculation in looking to the future.

Possibly the most important change that has occurred is a further loosening of party ties and a great increase in split-ticket voting. In 1968 the voters elected a Republican president while electing Democratic majorities in both the House and Senate. In the midterm election of 1970, Democratic majorities were again returned. In 1972, the Republican president was reelected by an overwhelming majority; and the voters once more returned Democratic majorities to House and Senate as they also did in 1974. In 1976, a Democratic president was elected by a narrow majority while the Democrats in Congress ran far ahead of him in most states. With the President's popularity at a relatively low ebb, large Democratic majorities in Congress were again returned in 1978.

The patterns of voting for Congress that we are seeing are in considerable part the result of the special characteristics of long-term party realignment in the formerly one-party states. The northern states that were essentially one-party Republican realigned in the direction of becoming competitive in 1932, but the process was far from complete that year with some reversion to Republicanism afterward. The realignment to competition in congressional voting mostly occurred in 1954 and 1956, and these states as a group have remained competitive in their congressional voting most of the time since 1956, with a corresponding decrease in their previous tendency to send mainly Republican members to Congress.[2]

The southern states that were one-party Democratic realigned sharply in presidential politics in 1948 and have been highly competitive in presidential politics since that time. But they did not begin to realign in congressional politics until after 1958; from 1958 through 1972 the trend line in Democratic voting in congressional and gubernatorial elections was steadily downward but did not reach the 50 percent mark.[3] Democratic representation in Congress from the South has been progressively reduced since 1958, but Democrats are still heavily in the majority in the southern representation.

Meanwhile, the amateurs have been having a field day in both parties. New types of political clubs have burgeoned in many parts of the country, especially in suburban areas.[4] A nationwide mobilization of amateurs with a heavy ideological motivation was largely responsible for the nomination of Senator Barry Goldwater by the Republican party in 1964, as it was also for that of Senator George McGovern by the Democratic party in 1972. Conflict between amateurs and professionals was a factor in the defeats that followed both of these nominations; and in each party a maturing process resulted that may be helpful in the future. The characteristically anti-organization attitudes of many amateurs have not been helpful to conceptions of party responsibility, but in both parties the amateurs have been intent upon more concern for national issues and stronger platform action.

Party unity in Congress has apparently continued to decline on the basis of some measurements, but the statistical decline seems to be largely the product of a sharper cleavage between the remaining conservative southern Democrats and other Democrats. According to a leading student of the subject,

If we eliminate the South and party agreement roll calls, the incidence of party voting in recent sessions has been high, considerably higher, in fact, than it was in the years 1921-44. Given these conditions, the positions of the two parties are particularly clear-cut on economic issues, monetary and fiscal policies, government action, housing, labor, and taxation. Indeed, in the North, on issues of this kind, the two parties approach quite closely the model of responsible party government. This statement could not have been made in 1951.[5]

Outside the South, there has been a growing tendency for the constituencies to reject representatives who looked like mavericks or insurgents in their respective parties.[6] Even in the South, liberal Democrats with a national orientation are beginning to be elected in some urban constituencies. As party realignment continues to spread in the South, along with urbanization and industrialization, this may be increasingly the case for the Democrats who can survive.

The institutional changes that have occurred since 1950 have included some modest reversals of previous changes. Little or no further spreading of open primaries has occurred since 1950. Cross-filing was abolished in California in 1958 after a campaign in which the Report of the Committee on Political Parties was a modest factor.[7] The so-called challenge primary, in which no primary is held unless the nomination of a political convention is strongly objectionable, has begun to spread and is finding some favor among reform groups that were rather strongly antiparty in an earlier day. Various forms of pre-primary endorsement have survived or arisen, in part as a by-product of the club movement in some states.

Between 1968 and 1972, the McGovern-Fraser Commission on Party Structure and Delegate Selection was at work in the Democratic party. Its 18 guidelines for delegate selection, produced in 1970, were thereafter the basis for revising party rules substantially in all states.[8] Most of the guidelines related to obviously needed reforms and were not controversial. Those that looked to increased representation for women, young people, and blacks were clearly controversial, and did bring a considerable increase in the representation of all three groups. One guideline prohibited the ex-officio designation of delegates and brought on a reduction in the number of party officials who served as delegates in 1972. Objections to this change were so sharp that a reversal has been occurring in the national convention of 1976 and the midterm conferences of 1974 and 1978. Perhaps the most important result of the McGovern-Fraser Commission experience was the demonstration that the parties can take national action that can be enforced on the state parties, a sign of the nationalization of politics that has been occurring in many other ways.[9]

Other reform efforts brought a new formula for the apportionment of votes among the states at the Democratic National Convention of 1972, a formula that put nearly half of the apportionment on a basis of an average of the party's share of the popular vote in the last three presidential elections, with the remainder allocated among the states on the basis of their electoral college strength. No such change was adopted in the Republican party, but it was in the federal courts on the issue even before the convention, as it continued to be for some time thereafter. The Supreme Court eventually decided not to intervene, in a decision that strengthened the control of the parties over their own affairs. The convention committees were also restructured at the Democratic convention of 1972 on a fair apportionment basis, and the Democratic National Committee has been comprehensively revised on a mixed plan, part of which parallels the revision of the convention committees, and the remainder of which mainly gives representation on the committee to the state party chairmen and the highest ranking state officers of the opposite sex. The platform drafting process in the Democratic party was also substantially revised in 1972 under new rules requiring that the proposed platform be completed and distributed to the delegates before they leave their homes to come to the convention. This practice was followed again in 1976 when the platform was heavily influenced by presidential candidate Jimmy Carter, but was also influenced by the congressional forces within the party.

Several changes have occurred in Congress.[10] By a series of steps and with accumulating changes in its membership, the Rules Committee of the House has been changed from a recurring obstacle to a facilitator of legislation; formerly responsive to the conservative coalition for most of a generation, it no longer is. In the Senate, where the filibuster prevented civil rights legislation for many years, filibusters were successively broken in 1960, 1964, and 1965. The filibuster remains as a tactic, but no longer has the fearsome quality that once attended it. In the House, the Democratic Study Group has reached maturity, with two-thirds of the Democrats in the House as members, and has been increasingly effective in organizing liberal Democrats and achieving various reforms. The seniority rule for electing committee chairmen has been modified to require a record vote by secret ballot in the caucus. Three seniority chairmen were displaced by caucus voting after the elections of 1974.

Perhaps most important of all, the House Democratic caucus has been meeting regularly since 1969 to discuss legislation and has become increasingly important as a forum in which party policy is worked out.[11] A similar shift occurred among House Republicans at an earlier date, and the party conferences have also become increasingly important in the Senate. Congress, at least, has been moving back in the direction of party responsibility for the program.

For the last several years, however, much of the literature on political parties has been sounding cries of alarm over "The Onward March of Party Decomposition"[12] and the tendency of other agencies to replace the parties in the mobilization of the voters.[13] Processes of party weakening seemed to reach a new level in the elections of 1978.[14] The candidates for Congress and the governorships used more television advertising than ever before, establishing their own direct contacts with the voters, who in turn were acting more like observers at a sporting event than participants in an election. Candidates were able to spend more money than ever before, much of it their own money, as the result of the Supreme Court ruling some years ago that struck down limits on candidate expenditures. Political action committees (PACs) have proliferated under the present campaign finance laws; many candidates received multiple contributions of $5,000 each from as many different PACs. It was a campaign of loners, in which every candidate seemed to be in business for himself. Grass-roots campaigning by knocking on doors was less important than formerly. The influence and

Paul T. David

contributions of the political parties, both financial and organizational, seemed to reach a low ebb, with the press and media commenting with unusual unanimity on the disintegration of party structures.

There is no doubt that the parties and the party system are in a difficult period of transition, which seems to be marked most of all by a weakening of the relationship between the parties and the voters and the relationship between the parties and their elected officeholders. Yet as the previous pages have indicated, there have been occasional signs of revitalization, mainly in the work of the national party conventions and their reform commissions and in party organization in Congress. It may be that further attempts to restore party vitality are most likely to arise in the party groups in Congress—and possibly also in the White House.

David Broder, one of the most acute students of the problem, recently offered some pungent comments:

> American politics has reached the point where it has to get worse before it can get better. Specifically, it must become more painful and difficult for officeholders. And because single-interest groups are making it more painful and difficult, they are helping create the conditions in which responsible politics and government may be reborn. . . .
> More and more officeholders are demanding protection from what one of them has called the "issues extortionists." They are asking why there is nothing to provide some defense against this cross fire of nonnegotiable special-interest demands.
> The blunt answer is that they themselves helped destroy the one institution that historically filled that function—the political party. The officeholders are now being victimized by people who have borrowed their own campaign techniques to use against them.
> My guess is that few candidates or officeholders are ready to sacrifice their own freedom of action to rehabilitate their party. But it may be that when more of them . . .

The lesson the officeholders have to learn was stated at the beginning of the republic by Benjamin Franklin: Either they hang together or they hang separately.
Give them a few more years of the rigors of single-shot candidacies and single-issue movements, and even the dullest politicians will discover the need to reinvent political parties.[15]

Perhaps the best illustration of Broder's position on party decay is the timidity with which the Democratic party has approached the holding of midterm conferences. The holding of such conferences was one of the recommendations of the Committee on Political Parties. They were envisioned as a campaign rally to start off the midterm campaigns and a place to write an updated party platform on which the party's candidates for Congress could all run. But after the 1972 national convention had mandated a midterm conference in 1974 to consider the proposed party charter, it was finally agreed to hold the conference only after the election, lest it embarrass some Democratic candidate in his local campaign. The charter as adopted in 1974 looked to the possibility of further midterm conferences, and again it was decided to hold one in 1978. But again the forces of timidity—probably both executive and legislative—brought on the holding of the conference only after the election, leaving the whole enterprise without much point. A conference in May or June of the midterm election year that comprehensively addressed the issues confronting the party and prepared a new platform would be a scene for serious negotiation among all elements of the party, including the president when the party has one and the party's members of Congress. Nothing else could more clearly embody the party's concern for program, and the absence of such a conference is one of the clearest demonstrations of the general reluctance of the parties to move toward more responsibility for the conduct of the government.

Yet the parties are not actually dead, even if moribund. It may be years before there is again as strong a move toward party reform as the one that started in 1968. On the other hand, having learned how to use reform commissions and the extent to which they can be effective, it may be that one party or the other, or even both, will soon begin to seriously confront the issues of more effective government and the relationship of the parties to that goal. The reform commissions we have had so far, so active in the Democratic party, less so in the Republican, have not been much concerned with executive-legislative relations and the issues of party responsibility that underlie them. But the time may come when future reform commissions will turn their attention in that direction. In that case, the old 1950 Report of the APSA Committee on Political Parties will again be a prime source for renewed attention and ideas on the problem as a whole and on many of the specifics. It will not have been written in vain.

NOTES

1. "Single Issue Politics," *Newsweek*, 6 November 1978, 42–52 (Australian edition).

2. Paul T. David, *Party Strength in the United States 1872–1970* (Charlottesville: University Press of Virginia, 1972), 42.

3. *Ibid.*, 45.

4. James Q. Wilson, *The Amateur Democrat* (Chicago: University of Chicago Press, 1962).

5. Edward V. Schneier, Jr., revised edition, Julius Turner, *Party and Constituency: Pressures on Congress* (Baltimore: Johns Hopkins Press, 1970), 245.

6. *Ibid.*, 227–29.

7. The Report was one of the items cited in a campaign pamphlet.

8. Commission on Party Structure and Delegate Selection, *Mandate for Reform* (Washington, D.C.: Democratic National Committee, 1970), 34–35.

9. Paul T. David, "Reform Efforts Continue On State Party Structures," *National Civic Review*, 61, May 1972, 226–31; "Political Parties Continue Struggle for Reform," *National Civic Review*, 62, March 1973, 118–24.

10. Lawrence C. Dodd and Bruce I. Oppenheimer, eds., *Congress Reconsidered* (New York: Praeger Publishers, 1977); Stephen K. Bailey, *Congress in the Seventies* (New York: St. Martin's Press, 1970).

11. "Democratic Study Group: A Winner on House Reforms," *Congressional Quarterly Weekly Report*, 31 (2 June 1973), 1366–71.

12. W. Dean Burnham, *Critical Elections and the Mainsprings of American Politics* (New York: W. W. Norton, 1970), Ch. 5.

13. Frank J. Sorauf, *Party Politics in America*, 2nd ed. (Boston: Little Brown & Co., 1972), Ch. 17.

14. For easy source material on this, see the post-election analyses in the issues of *Newsweek* and *Time* after the election of 1978; but similar commentaries were carried widely in the press and on the media throughout 1978.

15. David S. Broder, "Let 100 Single-Issue Groups Bloom: The Pains They Cause May Push Politicians Back to the Parties," *Washington Post*, Sunday, 7 January 1979, Outlook section. See also Broder's book, *The Party's Over: The Failure of Politics in America* (New York: Harper and Row, 1972), especially Ch. 11 on the continuing need for more party responsibility.

CHAPTER ELEVEN

Government as Agent of Social Change: Some Problems in Theory[*]

PAUL T. DAVID

To write an essay that attempts to consider problems of theory in the general area of the relationships between government and social change is a formidable assignment. The present essay became possible only because it reflects ideas that have been developing in a graduate seminar that I conduct with Professor William S. Weedon under the title: "Processes of Change: Their Origins, Interaction, and Governmental Consequences."[1] The students include doctoral candidates in government and foreign affairs, together with mid-career executives from a diverse range of federal bureaus and field services. The seminar is accordingly oriented to the processes of change that are of importance to the statesman, the public administrator, and the political scientist.

---

[*]*Presented at an Arden House conference sponsored by the Columbia University School of Social Work entitled "The Role of Government in Promoting Social Change" on 18–21 November 1965 in Harriman, New York, with Murray Silberman as conference director and editor, and Thomas Fred Lewin as conference chairman. Reprinted with permission.*

It is deliberately interdisciplinary in its range and is concerned as much with social change and economic change as with political change. We have found it necessary to develop our own system of categories for the study of processes of change. It would be presumptuous to say that we have developed a general theory of the processes of change that are having their effect in the contemporary world but we are moving in that direction.

The system of ideas we have been developing is comprehensive in its structure and broad in its coverage. Conversely, it is undoubtedly sketchy and thin where dealing with many problems and areas of primary concern to professional students of social work and sociology. As a general system of ideas about change, it may have some usefulness in giving a broadly orienting perspective.

Hence this paper begins with a brief discussion of the major processes of contemporary change before turning more specifically to conceptions of social change and the functioning of government as an agent of social change.

PRIMARY SOURCES AND PROCESSES OF CHANGE

Basic to our approach has been the assumption that the major processes of contemporary change are relatively few in number and that each has characteristics giving it identity and a degree of autonomy, despite the complexity of the interaction among the processes and the resulting appearance of overlap and confusion.

This is an assumption of considerable importance for theory construction and it has not gone unchallenged. It is easy to argue that the processes of contemporary change are numerous beyond counting, that they vary in significance, that they continually interact, and that the degree of overlap is so great that any separateness of identify is a fiction. The concept of process is itself only vaguely understood, although by implication it is what goes on in any system of action in the functioning of variables that have a continuing or recurrent relationship to each other. One definition of process is simply "Any phenomenon which shows a continuous change in time; as, the process of growth."[2]

Paul T. David

Complex systems of action can undoubtedly be dissected into more than one set of processes in which the terms are coordinate and comparable. For our purposes in attempting to understand what is going on in the contemporary world, it seems possible to identify four major categories:

1. Growth processes and their concomitants
2. Innovative processes of science, technology, and invention
3. Ideological processes: belief systems and their impact
4. Conflict processes: war, revolution, and mass conflict.

Each of these four categories of process seems primitive, distinctive, and coordinate. All are producers of change whether change is desired or not. They may be influenced, controlled, directed, or conceivably stopped completely in some circumstances, but to the extent that they operate, change will occur. In our seminar we have not been concerned with whether the resulting change is primarily social change, as distinguished, for example, from economic change or political change; it would seem to be self-evident that all four of these processes do indeed produce social change on a scale putting each in the first order of importance for the analysis of change in social systems.

Each of the four categories seems to involve distinctive internal mechanisms of causation that must be understood if the category as a whole is to be understood. Growth processes in particular are fundamental to every form of living organism and to every population of living organisms. In studying growth processes, we begin with growth in the human population because it is socially the most primitive and for some purposes the most important. Economic development is taken next because it includes not only population growth but all of those economic accumulative processes that involve the "compound interest principle."

As economies grow, they shift in composition; the shift runs mainly from agriculture to industry to the service trades and professions.[3] A corresponding reallocation of the population among occupations is the result, with economic and social restratification trailing along in the wake of occupational restratification. Urbanization is in turn brought on by industrialization and the accompanying migrations and occupational restratifications. All forms of growth and their concomitants bring pressures on natural resources and the physical environment that have recently become painfully evident; meanwhile elements of the population are left behind in all of this movement to form the hard core of the poverty problem.[4]

The innovative processes of science, technology, and invention involve a type of creation in the first instance that is almost akin to the biological function of mutation. A genuine scientific or technical innovation that persists has the effect of setting in motion a type of process that is quite different from the accumulative aspects of growth. Innovation of this kind was a prime subject of interest to William F. Ogburn, who regarded it as the principal source of social change, a somewhat culture-bound view that was developed at length in his book *Social Change* and that may have been moderately correct for the American culture during his lifetime.[5] Even now, there is a tendency to attribute all of the major changes of the present day to the heightened impact of science in this technological era. Technical innovations are measurably responsible for a considerable proportion of all economic growth in the United States. Furthermore, the most terrifying aspects of the world today are the result of the work of science in the field of military technology.

Ideological processes involving the creation and dissemination of new belief systems require innovation as much as science, technology, and invention, but any reference to ideological processes usually conveys a quite different meaning. Furthermore, it would seem that after the point of creation and initial formulation of a new belief system has been passed, the processes involving its dissemination and impact are sufficiently different from those involving the utilitarian aspects of the culture to make the difference completely recognizable. The distinction was defended specifically by Robert M. MacIver and Charles H. Page in their well-known textbook.[6] It is also noted occasionally by Richard T. LaPiere in his recent book, although in developing his basic theory that innovation is the source of all cultural and social change—a theory that has insufficient room for adequate attention either to growth processes or conflict processes—he makes little distinction between the processes of innovation, advocacy, and adoption as applied to material and nonmaterial innovation.[7]

Conflict processes were the fourth category previously referred to as embodying distinctive kinds of causation. Ideologies can produce conflict as can technical innovation and the processes of growth by which territorial limits are reached and exceeded. Conflict processes thus have many origins, in which any and all of the other processes may be involved; but a conflict process on the order of war, revolution, or mass conflict once in motion seems to have a logic of its own. Attempts to explicate that logic in all of its complexity are going on with more intensity than ever before.[8] On the face of things, it would seem that the causal relationships reflected in the outcomes of conflict processes have a special quality of unpredictability that sets them apart.

The four major categories so far identified seem in fact to arrange themselves along a spectrum of predictability. Growth processes, left to themselves in a fixed environment, would seem easily the most predictable, although even here prediction has many hazards. Innovative processes display a noticeable amount of recurrent pattern. Ogburn and his associates argued that prediction was possible to a considerable extent in the case of mechanical inventions and their consequences.[9] John Jewkes and his associates have argued strongly to the contrary.[10]

Ideological processes, mass movements, and the spread of new belief systems present an even more complex problem for anyone who wishes to predict, within the present state of the art. Who could have predicted accurately the future of Christianity in the year 200 A.D., or the Darwinian theory in 1870 (when Darwin himself seemed to be recanting), or communism in the year 1900? In each case something might have been said about climates of opinion, ideological compatibilities, and patterns of diffusion, but not much more.

Conflict processes by definition involve either a balancing of forces sufficient to give hope of victory to all parties, or views and positions that are held with such strength that they will be defended even at the cost of probable defeat. In the latter case, prediction may be possible; it certainly becomes difficult, if not impossible, in the former and much more important case. Yet the work of the

Government of the United States has been dominated by its involvement in conflict processes for the last 25 years, with no end in sight.

The four primary categories of process that have been under discussion here have been identified at a level of abstraction that may seem to leave them somewhere in the stratosphere, above the ordinary concerns of any professional group. Much of this quality of abstraction would rapidly disappear if there were time and space to discuss fully the subtopics within each of the four primary categories.

The basic theoretical problem in process taxonomy still remains. What is the best way to organize the universe of discourse on the processes of change in order to grapple with them effectively? The total subject must somehow be subdivided into parts bearing a visible and structural relationship to each other. The four primary processes identified have proved useful in the teaching problems that arise in programs of executive development for mid-career executives in the public service. They may have some utility in the further development of general theories of social change; but only the future can tell whether this view will come to be widely shared on an interdisciplinary basis within the social sciences.

PROCESSES OF CHANGE THAT TRANSMIT, MEDIATE, AND REGULATE THE PRIMARY PROCESSES

Our system of major processes of contemporary change includes three categories in addition to the four that have so far been discussed. These are:

1. Communicative and learning processes
2. Predictive and policy processes
3. Leadership and control processes

These all seem in some sense to transmit, mediate, and regulate the processes previously referred to. Collectively, they offer the means by which the primary sources of change might eventually be brought under some degree of self-consciously rational human control. They can also provide the mechanisms for taking the world down that road to serfdom of which we have been warned; historically, they have probably been used more often in the past either to maintain the status quo or to produce the less rational forms of conflict. But all three categories of process have sometimes operated systematically and persistently to produce change.

The double-barreled fashion in which each of the three final categories has been stated may suggest some lack of conceptual clarity. There is also some question concerning the separateness of their identities and the extent of their autonomy. But each has an identifiable set of institutions more or less peculiar to itself and each seems to involve noticeably different internal conceptions of causation even if a degree of overlapping is admitted. So far, the double terminology of each has been helpful in clarifying identity and in determining content.

A brief indication of the content of each may be helpful in clarifying the intent. Under communicative and learning processes, the matters subsumed in other disciplines under such terms as acculturation, socialization, cultural diffusion, and communication across social system boundaries are included. The entire apparatus of formal education, higher and lower, is a part of the category, along with its broadly conceived consequences and all of the rest of what Fritz Machlup has designated as "The Knowledge Industries."[11] We make what we can of the various theories concerning the mass media and mass communication as they affect both developed and developing countries.

The predictive processes are the newest category given separate treatment in our system. This fact testifies to our estimate of the growing importance of organized effort to foresee and predict in the world of today and tomorrow. Under this rubric a brief look can be taken at alternative views of the future, on which many eminent authors have recently written; both the extent and the potentialities of attempts at quantitative and nonquantitative prediction can be considered. Concepts of "planned" change in the world at large and the limits of rational decision making in human affairs are of special importance.

Finally, the seminar ends with the leadership and control processes. Here we consider the functions of leaders and how they may be controlled; the functions of law as social control; the domestic functions of governments as well as those in the international community, all in relationship to processes of change. This is the kind of ending that seems appropriate for a seminar held under the auspices of a political science department in a university; but there is no neglect of the issues that are clearly most relevant to the limits of what government can or should do, in contrast with other institutions in a pluralist society and world order.[12]

Provisionally, the three categories are treated as coordinate in importance with those previously discussed, at least for the future-oriented study of public affairs. Yet these categories are clearly different in a number of ways. In many respects they cut across the primary processes. They are less primitive, less autonomous. Whether they can be maintained as major terms in the future development of some general theory of social change remains to be seen, although they bear some resemblance to what Charles P. Loomis has called the "master processes" in his highly elaborated methodology for the analysis of social systems and social change.[13]

Our terms are broader, looser, and probably omit much of what any sociologist would consider essential for his analysis; they relate much more readily to the general concerns of humanity and to the literature in which those concerns have been given expression. The three categories seem heuristically useful to a high degree; it can be hoped that others will find them similarly useful, at least until something more nearly adequate replaces them.

WHAT IS SOCIAL CHANGE?

In the system of ideas so far discussed, it has not been necessary to set boundaries around particular forms of change that are considered "social change." Social work and sociology as professions are concerned with social change and with whether and how government might promote it. Hence there may be a need for a working definition of social change, or of the kinds of social change in which those engaged in social work and sociology should be interested.

The term *social change* has been in use for a considerable period, but it does not seem to have any commonly agreed meaning among those who use it most, the professional sociologists.[14] Good definitions of social change are rare. Generally it has been taken for granted as something already understood in the context in which it is being discussed. This was largely true even of Ogburn's work in the 1920s and 1930s.

After Ogburn, books on social change were out of fashion for a generation, presumably because of the prevailing emphasis on equilibrium processes in the analysis of social structure and function. The outstanding example of this was the work entitled *Toward a General Theory of Action*, by Talcott Parsons, Edward Shils, and seven other contributors. The theories of this book and of the dominant school in American sociology were concerned primarily with what goes on within a social system that is generally in a state of stable equilibrium. How social change might conceivably occur is explicitly discussed in about four pages in the middle of the book.[15]

General textbooks on sociology were compelled to give some attention to social change even during the period from 1930 to 1960 when the monographic literature on the subject was so thin. Probably the best treatment was the one in the textbook by MacIver and Page.[16] They took an eclectic view of the whole subject, while distinguishing between utilitarian and non-utilitarian changes in civilizations and cultures. Most of their work seems useful for the careful analysis of relationships between biological, technological, cultural, and social aspects of change. They used terminologies of their own that are now outdated, as in their attempt to define civilization as the utilitarian aspect of the culture, but their work can still be read with profit.

MacIver also published a major book, *Social Causation*, in 1942. In his preface he stated that "It can scarcely be doubted that if we could learn better how to investigate and how to interpret the phenomenon of social change the social sciences would advance to a higher level. This work is devoted to that cause."[17] This book apparently never went beyond a single printing in its hardback edition, although it would seem to be a work of utmost significance and usefulness for the logic of the social sciences. Fortunately, it has recently been republished in paperback, with a new introduction and a revision of its annotated bibliography.

In the mid-1950s, *Interpreting Social Change in America* by Norman F. Washburne was published in paperback.[18] The author was mainly interested in changes in social institutions which, he argued, were the best units of analysis in any attempt to explain how social change occurs in whole societies. He was inclined to consider "the overwhelming event" the principal agent of social change. He also discussed the impact of mechanical inventions, population movements, attrition of natural resources, and the actions of neighboring societies as agents of social change; he produced a useful bibliography that mainly revealed how little there was worth citing.

In recent years, sociology has been seeking a new mastery of the study of social change if one may judge from the "themes" that have been used in annual meetings of the professional sociologists and the less frequent world congresses. "Civilizations and Their Changes" was the announced theme of the 1965 meeting of the American Sociological Association. The meeting was said to have shown many signs of change in the direction of the interests of the profession, but was without substantial new contributions to any general theory of social change.[19]

A recently published book of readings carries the claim on its dust jacket that "The study of social change is in the vanguard of research in the social sciences today." But the editors comment, as they introduce their section on modern theories, that "The grand theories gave inadequate guidance for sociological research, but no modern theory of social change has replaced them."[20] They quote Wilbert E. Moore to the effect that "An 'integrated' theory of social change will be as singular or as plural as sociological theory as a whole, and will include about the same subdivisions and topics."[21]

Moore himself recently published a paperback entitled *Social Change* in which he suggests that he is "dealing with a subject where only fools rush in and authentic angels have not yet trod."[22] In this work, his conceptualization of social change seems to range all the way from minor readjustments within small groups to changes within the world community. At the annual meeting of sociologists, referred to above, he read a paper on "Global Sociology: The World as a Singular System" in which he argued that for some purposes the entire world could indeed be viewed as a single social system.[23]

Moore's recent work has been characterized by his preoccupation with the newly modernizing societies and the remarkably rapid processes of social change that are occurring in them. He commented that the equilibrium models of society are "relatively harmless" when used merely to call attention to society's "significant self-regulating mechanisms." But he continues, ". . . there are also ample sources of disorder in social systems, of tensions and conflicts, of *intrinsic* sources and paths of change [his italics]. . . . If an equilibrium model is taken at all seriously, these circumstances are downright embarrassing. . . . Social revolutions no longer just happen if they ever did. They are planned and executed, despite the real resistances that equilibrium models of society help to identify, but not to protect."[24]

At another conference, the question "What is Social Change?" was raised as part of a discussion of social systems and their analysis. A paper presented by Charles P. Loomis, summarizing theoretical elements of his two recent books, was the basis for discussion. Loomis defined social change "as the alteration in the systemic attributes of a society and its subsystems, through the development of new systems, the alternation of the old ones, or a combination of these two." He specified three stages as relevant primarily to directed change: "initiation in which an innovation is brought to the attention of the target system; legitimization, in which the change is evaluated as rightful; and execution, an act whereby systemic linkage is achieved by uniting the external pattern of the change agency system with that of the target system."[25]

Presumably the most important recent book on the subject of social change is the one by Richard T. LaPiere, previously referred to. Published in 1965, it seems to be the first comprehensive and systematic treatment of its subject in many years. LaPiere vigorously criticizes his colleagues for their inattention to the subject and develops his own theory at length. Many will undoubtedly disagree with major elements of that theory, but the book reflects an immense amount of scholarship and a lifetime of thought.

LaPiere views social change mainly as change in societies and in social systems, and comments "To constitute a socially significant change, the new must not only be adopted by a sufficient number of the members of a social population to give it currency, but so integrated into the social system that it will endure."[26]

A major intellectual issue that seems to be latent in many contemporary discussions is this: "Should social change be defined primarily as change in the personalities, conduct, and behavior of individuals that will adapt them more fully to the social systems in which they find themselves? Should it be defined as change in existing social systems at all levels that will adapt them more fully to the requirements of the individuals of whom they are composed? Or should there be genuine concern for both kinds of social change and its achievement on a basis involving some reconciliation of possibly conflicting objectives?" The answer to these questions bears directly on what role is possible or appropriate for government in the promotion of social change.

GOVERNMENT AS CHANGE AGENT IN THE SOCIAL SYSTEM

In what sense can, will, or should government serve as an agent of social change, whatever is used as the working definition? Is it within the limits of intellectual propriety to think of government as a "change agent" within the larger social system in which it is immersed? If not, why not? To what extent is government responsible for originating the various major processes of change that have been previously identified? To what extent must it respond to them, wherever they originate?

To give a series of short answers that may serve as first approximations, the following can be offered: If government governs, it will act as an agent of social change in all of the senses of that term, whether it wishes to or not. If government is responsive to the social order in which it finds itself, it will act as an agent of change in directions desired by that social order. Furthermore, it would seem more attractive to conceive of government as the servant rather than the master of society in acting as an agent of change. The problem of democratic government is the problem of making the more attractive conception a reality.

The extent to which government is responsible for the processes of change as previously reviewed would seem to vary across a wide spectrum. In the United States, the federal government has rarely been given much credit or much blame for initiation of the primary processes of change: growth, innovative, ideological, or conflict; although it has had a considerable responsibility for carrying along, maintaining, and regulating elements of these processes. More often it has seemed that government has responded to pressures for change rather than having initiated them.

Every government is made up of a collection of human beings, each of whom, at some time and under some circumstances, may have some capacity to initiate social change. Most obviously this is true of the President of the United States. It is clearly true of the members of the Congress, individually and collectively; of the ranking members of the executive branch; and of the members of the Supreme Court—as they have demonstrated in *Brown v. Board of Education* (1954) and other school segregation and civil rights cases of recent years. Surely *Brown v. Board of Education* was a case in which decisions of government indeed initiated a far-reaching sequence of social change. It would be difficult to find a case in which the role of government as agent of social change has been either more conspicuous or controversial.

Yet this case well illustrates the fact that every major governmental decision may be as much a response as an initiative. Inevitably a decision is part of a chain of events. To this extent a decision is a response, but it is also an initiative because it involves choice and some view of the future. Even if the choice seems foreordained, there is room for major differences of perception, both inside and outside the government, concerning what has been "foreordained." So long as government is manned by human beings, it can never be wholly neutral in either its perceptions or its decisions; it will always be important as an agent of social change.

The ways in which government can act in this way are manifold, but it is possible to distinguish at least three major patterns, each of which has its own importance. First of all, government may and does produce social change through the ultimate effects of its massive operational, construction, and military programs. In most of these cases, social change is more likely to be an incidental result than an intended purpose, although as government becomes more sophisticated in such matters, it may become more possible to avoid social change that is both unintended and dysfunctional.

The federal highway program, for example, was intended in the first instance simply to facilitate intercity travel by automobile. Its consequences as they have unfolded have included the development of the automotive manufacturing industries on a scale otherwise impossible, many changes in the patterns of industrial location, scattering of places of residence in relation to places of work, and many aspects of the whole complex of urban and suburban life as it currently exists in the United States.

Second, government produces social change through its handling of the central levers of influence and control with which the social and economic systems are increasingly equipped, a form of action that need not necessarily involve large bureaucratic staffs. Key decisions of the Supreme Court such as the one previously cited may be of this character. So is the deliberate use of fiscal policy to prevent unemployment and to foster economic growth.

The central core of economic doctrine in this area is usually attributed to a single brilliant innovator, the economist John Maynard Keyes. For the United States, the symbolic recognition of merit in his position came in the enactment of the Employment Act of 1946, declaring the responsibility of the federal government to promote "conditions under which there will be afforded useful employment opportunities, including self-employment, for those able, willing, and seeking to work, and to promote maximum employment, production, and purchasing power."[27] By 1956, President Eisenhower was referring to this act as "a charter to which all Americans can wholeheartedly subscribe."[28] Recently the basic mechanisms for maintaining control of the economy as a whole have been used with a degree of vigor from which it would seem future administrations will find it difficult to retreat. A return of economic conditions as depressed as those that prevailed from 1931 to 1941 seems impossible. If this is the case, a social change of genuine importance has indeed been initiated and achieved by the federal government of the United States.

Third, government may act specifically to initiate social change through the employment or subsidization of staffs who act as agents of change in target situations; for example, in the case of the home economics agent who seeks to introduce new patterns of family living in a rural county. This form of deliberately intended action to promote social change goes back at least as far as the land grants for common schools under the Land Ordinance of 1785, although the Morrill Act of 1862, establishing the land-grant colleges, is often considered a milestone of equal importance.

The New Deal period of Franklin D. Roosevelt brought on a burst of activities designed to promote social change directly and indirectly. The social security system that Roosevelt created survives, as does the soil conservation service and a frequently revised series of activities in public housing. The major youth programs of the New Deal, the Civilian Conservation Corps (CCC) and the National Youth Administration (NYA), disappeared soon after our entrance into World War II, along with various other relief and welfare programs of the depression years.

The federal government renewed its direct attack upon many problems of social change in the Kennedy administration, and these efforts have been greatly expanded and solidified under the Johnson administration. The Poverty Program has been the most conspicuous and in some ways the most controversial of these efforts, many of which are so recent that they do not yet lend themselves to any well-considered evaluation.

The origins of Kennedy's thinking on the Poverty Program are said to go back to the book entitled *The Other America* by Michael Harrington.[29] This is a graphic description of the several kinds of poverty that remain in our affluent society, but which are generally unobserved by most middle-class Americans because the concentrations of poverty—geographic, occupational, racial, and social—are in areas, neighborhoods, and social strata with which they seldom come in contact.

As the federal government attempts to cope with these problems on a broad scale and through the use of all or most of the agencies of our pluralist society, it encounters many layers of veto authority in state and local governments and in the public and private agencies of education and social welfare. Others have dealt much more fully with these problems than is possible here. It would seem, nonetheless, that in all of this welter of federal action to produce social change, there is a great need for a reemphasis on processes by which the citizen may participate and be heard—not merely the middle-class citizen with his established place in society, but the underprivileged and the impoverished, not all of whom are unintelligent and most of whom know a great deal about their environment that is not widely known in other circles.

This view was the basis for Section 202(a)(3) of Title II of the Economic Opportunity Act of 1964, under which the poor became entitled to be consulted in the local administration of the Poverty Program. This provision may not survive in its original form. Certainly it has been controversial and clearly it provoked strong opposition from mayors, political machines, and welfare agencies that consider themselves threatened by this unwelcome intrusion of a form of administrative democracy.[30]

Something of the kind nonetheless seems needed at all levels as the lives of citizens are administered more and more by governmental agencies. The fact that a provision like Section 202(a)(3) could be written and enacted by the Congress—even if it was done in a fit of absentmindedness—may prove in the end to be one of the more hopeful signs for a future in which ancient political values may yet prove to have some capability for survival.

At any rate, it would seem that the federal government is here to stay in this business of social change. Adaptation will be required at many levels, including the various legislative, executive, and judicial branches of the federal government. Some social theorists appear to believe that the needed adaptations are inherently impossible because of the inner drives of any large-scale organization.[31] If this is true, we face an unhappy future unless the rising tide of population can be turned back in this and other countries. Every major increase in population density seems to bring on its own requirements for more collective activity and more organization.

Inasmuch as the world has survived so long despite the pessimists of former days, no doubt it will continue to survive in one

Paul T. David

way or another. In this country, it can surely be expected that the services of an enlightened federal government will continue to be helpful in a major way as we move ahead.

NOTES

1. The seminar and its work are described more fully in a paper by the present author under the title "Processes of Change: Identification, Classification and Analysis for Purposes of Governmental Study," delivered at the 1965 annual meeting of the American Political Science Association, portions of which were drawn upon substantially in the preparation of the present paper. A revision of the paper referred to is forthcoming in *Public Administration Review*.

2. *Webster's New Collegiate Dictionary*, 2nd ed.

3. This process is clearly reflected in the long-term census statistics of industrializing countries. A classic discussion can be found in Colin Clark, *The Conditions of Economic Progress* (London: Macmillan, 3rd ed., 1957), pp. 720 at pp. 490–85.

4. Cf. Paul T. David, *Postwar Youth Employment* (Washington, D.C.: American Council on Education, 1943), 172.

5. William F. Ogburn, *Social Change with Respect to Culture and Original Nature* (New York: B. W. Huebsch, 1922). Reissued (New York: Viking Press, 1950).

6. Robert M. MacIver and Charles H. Page, *Society: An Introductory Analysis* (New York: Holt, Rinehart and Winston, 1949), at 498–506.

7. Richard T. LaPiere, *Social Change* (New York: McGraw-Hill, 1965), 556.

8. See especially Kenneth E. Boulding, *Conflict and Defense: A General Theory* (New York: Harper & Row, 1962), 349; and Quincy Wright's *A Study of War*, recently republished by the University of Chicago Press in unabridged form with an updating chapter and also in a

condensed edition as a paperback with an introduction by Karl W. Deutsch.

9. As in the opening sections of the report they prepared for the National Resources Committee, *Technological Trends and National Policy* (Washington, D.C.: Government Printing Office, 1937), 388.

10. John Jewkes, David Sawers, and Richard Stillerman, *The Sources of Invention* (New York: St. Martin's Press, 1961), 428.

11. Fritz Machlup, *The Production and Distribution of Knowledge in the United States* (Princeton University Press, 1962), 416.

12. Cf. the final chapter of Robert M. MacIver's *The Web of Government*, reissued as a Free Press paperback; and note also the article by Max Ways, "The Era of Radical Change," *Fortune*, May 1964, 113–15 et seq.

13. Charles P. Loomis, *Social Systems: Essays on Their Persistence and Change* (Princeton: Van Nostrand, 1960), 349; Charles P. and Zona K. Loomis, *Modern Social Theories: Selected American Writers* (Princeton: Van Nostrand, 1961), 720.

14. The remaining portions of this chapter draw in part upon materials prepared initially for a chapter entitled "Government as Initiator of Social Change," to be published in the forthcoming 1966 Yearbook of the National Council for the Social Studies.

15. See pp. 230–33 in the Harper Torchbook paperback edition of 1962.

16. *Op. cit.*

17. Harper Torchbook paperback ed., 1964, xv.

18. Originally published by Doubleday, but now a part of the Random House series of Studies in Sociology.

19. Natalie Jaffe, "Sociologists Find Efforts 'Archaic'," *New York Times*, 5 September 1965.

20. Amitai and Eva Etzioni, eds., *Social Change: Sources, Patterns, and Consequences* (New York: Basic Books, 1964), p. 503 at p. 75.

21. Wilbert E. Moore, "A Reconsideration of Theories of Social Change," *American Sociological Review*, Vol. XXV, December 1960, 810–18, final paragraph.

22. Englewood Cliffs, Prentice-Hall, 1963, pp. 120 at p. vi.

23. I am indebted to Professor Moore for a copy of the paper.

24. Wilbert E. Moore, "Editorial Introduction," in Charles P. and Zona K. Loomis, *op. cit.*, xxiii–xxiv.

25. *Interprofessional Training Goals for Technical Assistance Personnel Abroad* (New York: Council on Social Work Education, 1959), pp. 198 at p. 35.

26. *Op. cit.*, 66.

27. Stephen K. Bailey provides an excellent history of the origins of the act in *Congress Makes a Law*, now in Vintage paperback.

28. Gerhard Colm, ed., *The Employment Act: Past and Future, A Tenth Anniversary Symposium* (Washington, D.C.: National Planning Association, 1956), p. 203 at p. ix.

29. Available in Penguin paperback.

30. Charles E. Silberman, "The Mixed-Up War on Poverty," *Fortune*, August 1965, 156–61 *et seq.*

31. LaPiere puts this position very strongly; *op. cit.*, p. 69 and Ch. 13.

CHAPTER TWELVE

A Review of the Work at the Chicago Conference on International Aviation*
(From a Secretariat Point of View)

PAUL T. DAVID

INTRODUCTION

All of the Secretariat for the Conference on International Civil Aviation, held in Chicago, from 1 November to 7 December 1944, was provided by the United States, which had issued the invitations to the conference. Naturally much of the Secretariat came from the United States Department of State, but many were recruited from other agencies of the United States Government. The largest single contingent came from the Civil Aeronautics Administration in the Department of Commerce, in view of the extensive work expected on what became the technical annexes to the Chicago Convention. The secretary general of the conference was Dr. Warren Kelchner, chief of the conference division in the State Department, but the

---

*Written by invitation of the McGill University in Montreal, Quebec, and originally published in Annals of Air and Space Law, Vol. XIX, Part 1 (1994). Reprinted with permission.

technical secretary was Theodore P. Wright, administrator of civil aeronautics in the Commerce Department.

Originating from the Executive Office of the President, Bureau of the Budget, where I was a chief fiscal analyst, I was appointed to the position of secretary of Committee I in Chicago. My Budget Bureau assistant, Virginia C. Little, served as assistant secretary of Committee I and as secretary of its Subcommittee 2. Erwin R. Marlin of the Budget Bureau served as assistant secretary of Committee IV, Interim Council. The secretary of that committee was George C. Neal, chief legal officer of the Civil Aeronautics Board, who later became a law partner of the Hon. L. Welch Pogue when both returned to private life in mid-1946.

At the time of the conference, Pogue was chairman of the Civil Aeronautics Board, which reported directly to the President on the awarding of certificates for international airline operation from and to the United States. He was one of the most influential members of the United States Delegation at the conference. From the point of view of the foreign delegates who were interested in getting their eventual airline operations into the United States or in receiving service from any American airline reaching their country, he was obviously the man to see for private talks at Chicago. He was and is both a highly persuasive person and a highly skilled attorney.

His special competence was most evident at the conference in presiding as chairman over the deliberations of Subcommittee 2 of Committee I, Air Navigation Principles. That Subcommittee succeeded in updating the existing body of international air law, which had come mainly from the Paris Convention on Aerial Navigation of 13 October 1919. As noted in the introduction to the *Proceedings of the International Civil Aviation Conference*, the Subcommittee "was of considerable importance, not only because it covered practically the entire subject matter of the Paris and Havana Conventions but also because it provided the means by which the work of Committee II and its ten technical subcommittees on the so-called *annexes* could be implemented." That Subcommittee prepared Part I, Air Navigation, of the Convention on International Civil Aviation.

Anyone not familiar with the inner workings of the United States Government might well have been surprised at my presence at the conference. The Bureau of the Budget, from which I came, may seem an unlikely agency to have been involved in aviation policy. Actually, the Bureau, now renamed the Office of Management and Budget (OMB), had an interest in practically every activity of the United States Federal Government. It prepared the annual budget of the United States Government for the president, but it was also the place where every enrolled bill from the Congress stopped on its way to the president. Under the Constitution, those bills must ordinarily be signed or vetoed by the president within ten days. Bureau staff work on each bill, which involves the rapid collection of views of all agencies known to be interested, a review of those views, the Bureau's own analysis of how the bill fitted into the president's program, and a Bureau recommendation for signature or veto.

Every proposed certificate for an international route to be flown by an American airline, or for entry by a foreign airline, came from the Civil Aeronautics Board to the Bureau on its way to the president for approval or disapproval. At the Bureau, it received the same kind of staff work as an enrolled bill. During my years in the Bureau (1942-46), I did most of the staff work and wrote the initial draft of the Bureau memorandum on each of the international route certificates as they came along. At the time, I was probably the only qualified air transport economist on the Bureau staff, that having been the field in which my first book (*The Economics of Air Mail Transportation*) was published. The assignments came to me from the assistant director of the Bureau in charge of Legislative Reference, and the memoranda making recommendations went back to him for the Bureau director and the president. In many cases they went through unchanged.

I was involved in aviation policy in a number of other ways. Most importantly, when Assistant Secretary of State Adolf Berle formed the high level of Inter-departmental Committee on International Aviation in March 1943, with the approval of the president and the secretary of state, a working subcommittee was created under the chairmanship of Welch Pogue, of which, in turn, I was secretary. Within a few months the subcommittee and the principal committee put together recommendations that Adolf Berle summarized for the president. They were part of the basis for discussion when Roosevelt and Churchill turned to international civil aviation during their talks in Quebec, from 10 August to 25 August 1943. The President came back with a renewed interest in developing aviation policy, and I was asked to prepare memoranda for Berle on a number of subjects for his use in briefing the President. Thereafter, I was aware of the developments in the American and British positions and the Canadian proposals during the months leading up to the Chicago Conference, but not really aware of how much the President was continuing to take a personal interest. That whole story is well told by Dobson in his recent book just cited, which seems based on an extraordinary amount of research in British and American archives, as well as other sources.

Virginia Little was associated with me in most of the activities noted above. Her recent two years of graduate work at the Fletcher School of Law and Diplomacy were most helpful in filling in on some aspects of the work. So we both arrived in Chicago somewhat prepared for what we found ourselves doing as part of the Secretariat.

Life in the Secretariat

Although all members of the Secretariat, so far as I knew, were American officials or employees of the federal government, at the conference we were all supposed to take on the role of an international civil servant. That meant that we should avoid special contact with members of the United States Delegation and seek to be impartial in our relations with all delegates regardless of what country they represented. We were not supposed to be privy to the instructions of the United States Delegation except as we had become aware of them before coming to the conference. Dr. Warren Kelchner of the State Department had emphasized these points to us at a briefing of the intended Secretariat on 27 October 1944, while we were still in Washington. Some reiteration occurred at an organizing meeting of the Secretariat in Chicago, which occurred shortly before the official opening of the conference. So far as I was ever aware, there were never any complaints about the behavior of the Secretariat.

Paul T. David

We did of course read newspapers. The *Chicago Tribune* was the great morning newspaper of the Middle West, available to conference personnel daily at breakfast time. Historically and solidly Republican, it had been anti-administration from the first day of the Roosevelt administration. The *New York Times*, which prided itself on being an objective newspaper of record ("all the news that's fit to print"), was much more friendly to the administration. It also was available by breakfast time, coming from New York by air freight.

Both the *Chicago Tribune* and the *New York Times* assigned specific reporters to cover the conference from day to day: Frank Hughes in the case of the *Tribune* and Russell Porter for the *Times*. Both had front-page stories the day after the conference opened, and frequent stories thereafter, but rarely again on the front page. War news continued to dominate both newspapers, with the war actively continuing in both Europe and the Pacific.

On 4 November, the fourth day of the conference, the *Tribune* published a long front-page story headlined "Sellout of U.S. Air Rights at Parley Feared—Threat to Military Security Foreseen." The story was datelined Washington, D.C., 3 November, but contained material obviously originating in Chicago that involved leakage concerning conflict within the United States Delegation. High officials in Washington, both civil and military, were said to be shocked by the air rights that Adolf Berle had proposed to give away in his opening statement for the United States and by his emphasis on the need for reciprocity. Pan American Airways was said to have negotiated commercial rights in 60 foreign nations without the United States being required to concede a single reciprocal right. The British were said to be insisting on the continuation of a 50-50 division of North Atlantic traffic, although 80 percent of the traffic had been American and probably would continue to be so after the war.

The next day, the *Tribune* story by Frank Hughes on page 5 was headed, "Berle Refuses to Make Reply on Air Sellout—Gives Election as Excuse for Ignoring Charges." Hughes reported that the *Tribune's* story had "commanded more than usual attention at the conference." Berle authorized publication of the following statement: "I don't have to inform you gentlemen that there is a national election on and a campaign incident thereto, and that a certain local newspaper has taken a very vivid interest therein." According to Hughes, most of Berle's press conference remarks were "off the record," meaning that they could not be attributed to him. (The United States presidential election was scheduled for Tuesday, 7 November. Roosevelt was reelected.)

The above exchange has been included here mainly because it illustrated to the foreign delegates and the Secretariat alike the sharpness of the issue of whether Pan American Airways could prevail in its desire for a "chosen instrument policy." Juan Trippe, head of Pan American, was not at Chicago, but one of his closest associates, Sam Pryor, was. So also was Senator Owen Brewster, a member of the United States Delegation. Brewster had long been known as Pan American's most persistent friend in the United States Senate, where legislation intended to anoint Pan American as America's "Chosen Instrument" was actively pending. Berle traced the leak in the delegation "to Brewster, with Sam Pryor as the conduit to the newspaper. Berle reported his findings to Under Secretary of State Stettinius in irate terms that almost imputed treason to Pan American Airways."

As members of the Secretariat, we had all been a part of that audience, estimated at 700, filling the ornate ballroom of the Stevens Hotel at the plenary session opening the conference on Wednesday, 1 November. There we had heard Adolf Berle begin by reading President Franklin Roosevelt's welcoming statement, in which he appealed for a peace time regime of freedom for air commerce in which all could participate. Roosevelt ended his statement by saying "with full recognition of the sovereignty and juridical equality of all nations, let us work together so that the air may be used by humanity, to serve humanity."

The next day at the second plenary session, reports of the organizing committees were ready. Credentials were accepted without discussion or dissent, although the first pocket directory of the conference participants had identified the delegates of Costa Rica, El Salvador, Honduras, and Nicaragua as officials of Pan American Airways. Those designations disappeared from the quickly issued second version of the directory. Representatives of 54 nations were present.

Paul T. David

The Committee on Rules and Regulations reported various minor changes in the draft it had considered and dealt with two matters of possible controversy. One concerned the working languages of the conference. The use of Russian was no longer an issue, since the Soviet Union had decided not to participate, although its intended delegation had reached Winnipeg, Canada, before being recalled on 29 October 1944. According to Welch Pogue, it had been assumed that Russian would be an official language of the conference when the Soviet Union had been expected to participate. Members of a preparatory Russian delegation had been in Washington in June 1944 and had obviously expected to be at the conference. They wanted information primarily about the technical standards that might come out of the conference and that they might have to meet in flying outside their own borders. They had no interest in discussing political issues.

With the Russian language out of the way, the Executive Committee of the conference had recommended English as the only working language of the conference, and the Rules Committee agreed. The chairman of the French Delegation, Max Hymans, speaking in French, regretted this decision, stating that "all international conventions since 1815 have been drawn up in French, the universal language of diplomacy." He did not move for a formal amendment of the rules.

The second potentially controversial question was the extent to which meetings of the conference should be open to the press. An American position in favor of openness to the press, unlike that taken at Dumbarton Oaks and Bretton Woods, had been clarified in an Executive Committee recommendation to the effect that plenary meetings of the full conference and of its substantive committees should be open to the press, "unless otherwise decided," but that subcommittee meetings should be private to expedite the work. The Rules Committee so recommended.

A third recommendation, originally suggested by Canada, was for the transposition of Committee III on Multilateral Aviation Convention to Committee I, and the converse transposition of Committee I, Provisional Air Routes, to Committee III. The original ordering, as suggested by the United States, reflected the preconvention United States' view that early agreement on a postwar pattern of worldwide air routes was an important conference objective, whereas the drafting of a permanent multilateral convention was probably more than could be achieved. In the United States' opinion, the conference should limit itself to provisional arrangements during which a permanent multilateral treaty could be developed. But the Canadians had arrived with a complete draft of a permanent convention and argued that completing it would be necessary for guidance in developing provisional arrangements. This view had general appeal, and the United States conceded.

The Report of the Committee on Rules and Regulations was adopted unanimously without change. For me, as the previously intended secretary of Committee III, now Committee I, my job had suddenly become much more important.

The report of the Committee on Nominations was next. Most of it was obviously *pro forma* on what had previously been agreed: Berle for permanent president of the conference, Steenberghe of the Netherlands as chairman of Committee II, Technical Standards and Procedures, Berle himself as chairman of Committee III, Provisional Air Routes, and Guimaraes of Brazil as chairman of Committee IV, Interim Council. Lord Swinton, head of the United Kingdom Delegation, had been originally listed as chairman of Committee I, Multilateral Aviation Convention and International Aeronautical Body, but he had requested that John Martin of South Africa be substituted. At a second meeting, the Committee on Nominations had agreed to accept John Martin. Its report was adopted unanimously without discussion. Organizing meetings of the four substantive committees were scheduled for the following day.

Readers of an earlier draft if this manuscript, familiar with the literature on permanent international secretariats, have asked for some evaluation of the Secretariat at Chicago. Was it large enough? Was it qualified? Was it well organized? Was it desirable to have it all provided by the host government? Apparently the professional literature of international relations has almost never addressed questions of this kind about ad hoc secretariats of the sort assembled at Chicago.

Paul T. David

The conference went through three phases, each with different demands on the Secretariat. During the first phase, up until 12 November 1944, the Secretariat seemed well organized and was being used much as had been intended by the American authorities who had planned the conference. During that phase, the Secretariat was certainly large enough and about as well qualified as it could be for operations in new territory. The second phase was the period of the so-called ABC talks, lasting from 12 to 20 November, discussed later. Most of the Secretariat was inactive except for the ongoing technical work of Committee II. The third phase, after the ABC talks, from 20 November to 4 December, involved some finishing work in Welch Pogue's Subcommittee 2 of Committee I, but was otherwise concentrated in the Joint Subcommittee of Committees I, III, and IV, where Virginia Little and I found ourselves serving as assistant secretary and secretary. We were under a heavy overload throughout that period, but I do not believe we could have used help from elsewhere in the Secretariat. We did get real assistance from some members of the drafting committees who were qualified and helpful experts. Other members of the Secretariat were mostly unemployed during that period. Some may have been called home.

As for whether it was desirable for the host government to provide the entire Secretariat, with questions about its ability to internationalize itself, there probably was not much alternative during the conditions prevailing during the war and early thereafter. Any alternative would have been difficult and time-consuming, and probably would have increased the level of confusion during the conference.

Opening National Positions

After disposing of the organizing committee reports, the second plenary session, on 2 November, then turned to the statement of national positions. Berle led off with comparisons of the use of the air with the use of the sea, each "a highway given by nature to all men." He followed immediately with an assertion of "the rule that each country has a right to maintain sovereignty of the air which is over its lands and territorial waters. . . . But consistent with sovereignty, nations ought to subscribe to those rules of friendly intercourse which shall operate between friendly states in time of peace. . . ." He commented on the centuries of conflict before the doctrine of freedom of the seas attained general acceptance and expressed hope that freedom of intercourse by air would not be subject to any such long period of conflict. In what became a lengthy statement, he detailed the major points of the United States' position.

Lord Swinton of the United Kingdom followed and commented first on the general aspirations that had brought together so many countries at this widely representative conference. He referred to the British White Paper as a statement of the general principles that would combine national aspirations with international cooperation. In defense of those principles, he said, "Every nation, which aspires to be in the air will wish to have, and indeed will insist on it, in addition to its own internal traffic, a fair share of its external air traffic as well." As an example, he referred to the prewar agreement between the United Kingdom and the United States on trans-Atlantic service in which "we agreed to run the service on a 50-50 basis." The question of frequencies of scheduled service would come first, he thought, in any agreement between countries. There would be a need for national quotas, and for some control over rates "to avoid waste and to get rid of subsidies." He doubted the possibility of reaching agreement on the details of a permanent solution at this conference, but insisted on the need for interim arrangements, bearing in mind the military necessities of the war still going on.

Canada was next, with C. D. Howe as its spokesman. He began by stating: "An international air authority, established along the lines of the Civil Aeronautics Board of the United States, is the principal proposal which Canada places before this conference." He noted that the details of the Canadian proposal were widely known. A preliminary draft of an international air convention had been published by Canada on 17 March 1944 and had been debated in the Canadian Parliament. He discussed the principles involved and answered potential objections. The Canadian position, as he presented it, seemed somewhat intermediate between that of the United Kingdom and the United States.

Paul T. David

The Canadian proposal seems to have been the first to introduce the concept of the "four freedoms," which became so much of the jargon of the conference, and to which a fifth freedom, variously interpreted, was later added. In abbreviated form they were as follows:

1. Freedom of peaceful transit.
2. Freedom of nontraffic stop (to refuel, repair, or take refuge.)
3. Freedom to take traffic from the homeland to any country.
4. Freedom to bring traffic from any country to the homeland.
5. Freedom to pick up and discharge traffic at intermediate points.

After Canada and before recessing to meet again in the evening, Mexico and India were recognized for brief statements, and D. G. Sullivan was given the opportunity to present at some length the proposal of New Zealand for "an international organization to own and operate air-transport services on international trunk routes."

In the evening, Max Hymans of the French Delegation, a vice president of the conference, had been asked to preside. He opened the session by making a statement for his government, only recently reestablished in Paris. He recalled the French initiative in the creation of the first International Convention on Aerial Navigation in 1919, the usefulness of that treaty during the 20 years that followed, and the current need for modernizing and replacing it. To avoid the formation of rival air blocs, "all the nations invited here must have a reasonable share in air transportation."

Arthur Drakeford of Australia was recognized next and made a powerful statement supporting and amplifying on the proposal previously offered by New Zealand. He emphasized the geographic isolation of both countries and their consequent need for effective linkage with the rest of the world by a competent air transport authority. He noted the security needs of both countries, in which aviation could be a major threat, and referred to their close association with the United States in fighting the war in the Pacific. Both Sullivan and Drakeford were speaking for Labour governments and there was undoubtedly sympathy for their views within the Labour party in Great Britain.

Other delegations heard from included Poland, Brazil, Panama, and Norway. Morgenstierne of Norway spoke especially for the countries devastated, and in some cases, like his own, still occupied by the aggressors. He hoped for early restoration of his country's rightful place in a peacetime world and expressed appreciation for the American offer to make suitable civil air transport airplanes available to friendly nations as soon as the military situation permitted.

In a wrap-up piece about the conference in the *New York Times* of Sunday, 5 November, Russell Porter predicted that the main problem of the conference would be to reconcile the British and American positions. He ended by concluding that if an international authority could be established, "its chief functions would be in establishing and maintaining uniform technical standards, including landing signals, weather reports, quarantine, and the like."

Committee Work

As scheduled, the four major committees of the conference met on Friday, 3 November.

Committee II, Technical Standards and Procedures, was assumed to have the least controversial assignment, but also the biggest workload in terms of the subjects on its agenda and the number of prospective subcommittees to deal with them. Those subcommittees were obviously in need of technically qualified chairmen and members. There was some doubt about the number of such persons among the conference delegations, although every delegation was entitled to be represented on every subcommittee if it so desired.

In opening the organizing meeting, Chairman Steenberghe of the Netherlands expressed appreciation of the honor given to his country, one of the pioneers of international civil aviation. On roll call, 45 of the 54 countries at the conference were found to be represented, 9 absent. The committee agreed almost immediately on the creation of ten subcommittees, eight of which had been the subject of preparatory work by the United States. Canada secured agreement on including the other two, one on Search and Rescue and Investigation of Accidents, the other on Publications and Forms. Edward Warner, representing the United States, pointed out that most of the subcommittees would be involved with publications and forms. Hence, it was agreed that the Subcommittee on Publications and Forms would have mainly a coordinating function in regard to recommendations originating elsewhere. It did not prepare a technical annex, but its recommendations on standardization where possible were reflected in the final report of Committee II.

When the item on submittal of draft annexes was reached on the organizing agenda, Edward Warner made a statement concerning the drafts the United States was prepared to submit. He referred to time pressures during their preparation, said they were not in any final state and were not to be taken as commitments of any United States' position. He noted the work of the International Commission for Air Navigation (ICAN) but observed that so much had happened in recent years that it was necessary to start afresh, without attempting to revise any existing text.

Chairman Steenberghe expressed thanks for this preparatory work, which clearly had not been duplicated elsewhere. Lord Swinton of the United Kingdom said the work was extraordinarily helpful and would save the conference weeks of time, in view of the encyclopedic knowledge and thoroughness of Edward Warner. Warner expressed appreciation for the kindness of those present, but noted the amount of work in various United States agencies that had gone into the drafts as presented.

The committee then adjourned for the weekend, giving time for the nomination of subcommittee chairmen and members. Some delegations sent home for additional technical help if it could be provided.

At the second meeting of Committee II on Monday, 6 November, 33 countries were represented. It was quickly agreed, on motion by France, that the secretary general of the prewar organization (CINA or ICAN), Albert Roper, be invited to attend committee and subcommittee meetings as an adviser when he so desired. A partial list of subcommittees and their chairmen was read, and the nomination of additional chairmen and members was requested.

Thereafter many of the subcommittees started meeting immediately; the roster of subcommittees was completed, each met frequently, and by 17 November, each completed a report. The full committee then met in a third plenary session on 18 November.

At that meeting, resolutions on Draft Technical Annexes and on the metric system that eventually appeared in the Final Act of the conference were debated, amended, and adopted. The first, on the status of the draft annexes, provided for the immediate and continuing study of the drafts by the participating states, who were to produce any proposals for revision by 1 May 1945 and were meanwhile urged to accept recommended practices as far and as rapidly as feasible. In its original form, this resolution had come out of the Steering Committee of the conference, had been published in the *Journal* of the conference for general information, and was presented to Committee II for approval by Edward Warner. A discussion between FitzMaurice of the United Kingdom and Warner resulted in some agreed redrafting, and the resolution was then adopted.

The resolution on the metric system as originally proposed by the Netherlands would have required the universal use of the metric system throughout international civil aviation. This brought on an extended discussion of the feasibility of the proposal in different technical fields. Eventually there was agreement on the amended form in the Final Act, with both metric and English systems of measurement to be used where needed, but with the whole matter subject to further study by the Provisional Organization.

Also at the third plenary meeting of Committee II, each of the ten subcommittee chairmen reported on the work of their subcommittees. An inquiry was made as to the need for a drafting committee to prepare the committee's final report, and it was agreed that this task should be entrusted solely to Edward Warner as the reporting delegate for the committee. The task was urgent, since the report would need the attention of both Committees I and IV of the conference.

As many readers are no doubt aware, Edward Warner became the first and only president of the Council of PICAO, and then the long-term president of the ICAO Council. Similarly, Albert Roper served from the beginning as secretary general of PICAO and then of ICAO for many years.

At the fourth and final plenary session of Committee II on 23 November, a draft report, with all of the subcommittee reports attached, was amended only in respect to the composition of technical committees of the Provisional Organization and then adopted. The committee was thus the first in the conference to complete its work, and the only one close to finishing within the time frame originally intended. The draft technical annexes it had prepared ran to some 188 pages on 12 subjects in the *Proceedings*, as follows:

Annex A. Airways System
Annex B. Communications Procedures and Systems
Annex C. Rules of the Air
Annex D. Air Traffic Control Practices
Annex E. Standards Governing the Licensing of Operating and Mechanical Personnel
Annex F. Log Book Requirements
Annex G. Airworthiness Requirements for Civil Aircraft Engaging in International Air Navigation
Annex H. Aircraft Registration and Identification Marks
Annex I. Meteorological Protection of International Aeronautics
Annex J. Aeronautical Maps and Charts
Annex K. Customs Procedures and Manifests
Annex L. Search and Rescue, and Investigation of Accidents

Committee III, Provisional Air Routes, with Adolf Berle serving as chairman, convened on 3 November. In opening the meeting, Berle emphasized that as soon as hostilities ceased, there would be a need around the world for civil air transport service. Pending the coming into force of any multilateral arrangement, bilateral, trilateral, or quadrilateral agreements would be needed among the countries concerned. In turn, there would be a need for general principles to guide such agreements as far as possible.

After discussion, the committee agreed to constitute Subcommittee I, Standard Form of Provisional Air Route Agreements. Ambassador Morgenstierne of Norway was appointed chairman of the subcommittee, and it met in organizing sessions on 4 and 8 November. The Netherlands delegate, F. C. Aronstein, was appointed reporting delegate and G. G. FitzMaurice of the United Kingdom was appointed draftsman to work on a standard form, in cooperation with Aronstein.

At a meeting on 9 November, Adolf Berle thanked the group for agreeing to start discussion of an American text and Lord Swinton of the United Kingdom agreed that bilateral agreements would be needed during an interim period beginning as soon as military operations ceased. Discussion then ensued on many points in the American draft, but no votes were taken. The subcommittee adjourned to await policy decisions elsewhere in the conference.

The subcommittee reconvened on 26 and 29 November to consider a text prepared by a drafting committee consisting of Aronstein, FitzMaurice, and delegates from Panama, Mexico, and the United States. (Cuba and Mexico had submitted a proposed alternative to the United States Proposal.) With much amending at both meetings, the final text was produced of what became Resolution VIII in the Final Act, the recommended "Standard Form of Agreement for Provisional Air Routes." The subcommittee having thus finished its work, Adolf Berle proposed that it adjourn and immediately reconvene as a plenary session of Committee III. In that session, which lasted about five minutes, the report of the subcommittee was approved and referred to the forthcoming plenary session of the conference.

At the opening session of Committee III, Berle had suggested that an understanding of the geography of the air routes most desired for operation at the cessation of military operations, and until a multilateral treaty was in force, would be of great value to the committee in completing its tasks. This brought on queries concerning whether the negotiation of such routes was intended as part of the work of the conference. Berle responded that the conference would have no such jurisdiction; that it was a matter for the countries concerned. However, he suggested that the Secretariat of the committee be authorized to accept and distribute such statements as any country might wish to make on the routes it might wish to fly during the interim period.

This was accepted by the committee and led to the remarkable collection of "International Route Proposals." Twenty-seven countries made presentations, many quite elaborate. The United States listed 20 proposed international routes going out from that country, most of them with multiple destinations, probably confirming the worst of British fears. Australia, New Zealand, Canada, South Africa, and the United Kingdom were notably absent from the listings. The conference did nothing officially about the listings except make them available to delegates as conference documents.

It seems clear that Committee III, in the form originally intended by the United States, would have been a much more important part of the conference than it was allowed to be. In the invitations to the conference, sent out on 11 September 1944, the proposed first objective of the conference was stated to be "the establishment of provisional world route arrangements by general agreement to be reached at the conference. These arrangements would form the basis for the prompt establishment of international air transport service by the appropriate countries."

In Berle's opening statement at the Second Plenary Session, he referred to this objective: "As the United States conceives it, this will be the work of the Committee on Provisional Routes. If its work is well done, I hope that we shall be able at the close of the Conference to report a great number of agreements between the interested countries, which, taken together, shall thus establish a provisional route pattern capable of serving the immediate needs of the world...." At the organizing meeting of Committee III, however, it was clear that Berle had retreated from any conference discussion of a world route pattern, presumably because of the strong objections of the British and Canadians to any such attempt. But Berle left open the possibility of private discussion of routes among the countries represented at the conference, and much discussion of that kind undoubtedly occurred. Welch Pogue has said that he was involved in many such discussions on behalf of the United States.

A Review of the Work at the Chicago Conference

Committee IV, Interim Council, held its organizing meeting on 3 November under the chairmanship of Hahnemann Guimaraes of Brazil. The chairman expressed confidence that the committee could plan the establishment and functioning of the proposed Interim Council "separately from the determinations of other Committees." Two subcommittees were authorized, one on the composition and organization of the Interim Council, the other on its powers and duties.

The first subcommittee organized promptly and immediately found much disagreement with the United States proposals on the composition and organization of the Interim Council, which would have given two memberships in a council of 15 to each of the United States, the U.S.S.R., the British Commonwealth of Nations, and one each to Brazil, China, and France, with six others to be elected, three from Continental Europe, two from the Western Hemisphere, and one from Asia or Africa. This matter was taken up next in a joint meeting of the two subcommittees on 10 November, at which a counterproposal by Cuba and Mexico was presented. It provided for an Assembly of all member states with equal voting powers, and for a council of 15 members freely elected by the Assembly. The Cuban-Mexican proposal was supported at the meeting by delegates representing 17 states in addition to its sponsors, most of them Latin American. The delegate from the United States expressed full support for the principle of juridical equality of all states, and offered no objection to the elimination of weighted voting in the council. The chairman suggested the need for a drafting committee, which was agreed and the meeting adjourned.

The next day, the *Chicago Tribune's* story by Frank Hughes, was headed "Small Nations Given Equality in Rule of Air—Latin American Proposal Wins at World Parley." The United States agreement to drop weighted voting in the Interim Council was announced by Chapa of Mexico and Machado of Cuba, who were said to be leaders of a bloc of 19 Latin American countries. They were quoted as saying that "the Latin American nations favored the American idea that any such international body should be advisory, with regulatory authority confined to technical matters."

Paul T. David

The second subcommittee on the powers and duties of the Interim Council met on 8 and 13 November. It worked mainly on the relevant provisions of the United States proposal, with many suggestions for amendments, including the use of "Provisional Organization" instead of Interim Council where relevant. Again further work was referred to the drafting committee.

No further meetings were held until 23 November, when another joint meeting of the two subcommittees was held, with Chairman Guimaraes presiding. He noted completion of the report of Committee II and the new document resulting from the tripartite talks involving the United States, Canada, and the United Kingdom. He proposed that the drafting committee should take account of these developments.

He noted three points for further determination by the conference as a whole: "namely, the location of the seat of the Interim Council; the election of members of the Council; and the apportionment of the expenses of the organization among the member States." This was accepted by those present. The existing report of the drafting committee then went back to the drafting committee with many amendments. At a final meeting on 29 November, the draft of an "Agreement to Establish the Provisional International Civil Aviation Organization" was given several amendments and approved. That ended the separate work of Committee IV, but it had produced the basis for what became known as PICAO.

Special Problems of Committee I

Committee I, Multilateral Aviation Convention and International Aeronautical Body, organized on 3 November under the chairmanship of John Martin, a "Co-delegate" of the chairman of the South African Delegation. It is taken last in this review because of the political complexity of its assignment. It had before it the four major proposals with which the conference had opened: the Australia-New Zealand proposal for an international authority to own and operate all international air transport services, a revised draft of the Canadian proposal for an International Air Convention, the British White Paper of 8 October 1944, and the United States' proposal of a Convention on Air Navigation.

John Martin (1884-1949) was an interesting personality and one of the most effective chairmen of a large and contentious meeting I have ever encountered. He deserved more credit than he has ever received for his part in bringing the Chicago Conference to an agreed conclusion after the situation he inherited from the ABC talks. Born in Scotland, he had a worldwide education as a child while his father moved from country to country, including even a period in the public schools of Chicago. Limited by poor eyesight in his youth, he never attended university. Early on, he joined an uncle in South Africa. He soon reached the position of advertising manager for the *Johannesburg Star* and thereafter advanced through stages to the head of the Argus Printing and Publishing Company. Under him, "it became the giant of the South African newspaper industry." He added important positions in the mining industry: the combination, said "to make him for two decades one of the most influential men in South Africa," was ended apparently by oncoming ill health in 1947. Meanwhile, he had performed important governmental services, including participation in the Empire civil air conferences in London in 1943 and Montreal in 1944 and then the Chicago Conference.

As a preliminary to the consideration of any of the four proposals, Chairman Martin suggested the need for general agreement on the importance of international cooperation in regard to civil aviation and for an appropriate international organization to facilitate it. A resolution to that effect was passed unanimously. The chairman then suggested approval for three subcommittees:

1. International Organization,
2. Air Navigation Principles, and
3. Air Transportation Principles.

These were eventually approved, but without much clarification of their respective functions and relationships.

Sullivan of New Zealand pressed repeatedly for a decision on when the proposal he favored could be taken up and objected to having it referred to a subcommittee. The result was the convening of a second plenary session, open to the press, on Wednesday, 8 November. There Sullivan presented his formal resolution, moved for its adoption, and defended it at some length. Drakeford of Australia followed to second the resolution and to rebut so far as he could objections to it.

The chairman then read a statement handed in by Brazil, in which there was appreciation for the purposes intended by New Zealand and Australia, but no possibility that Brazil could accept their proposal. It was suggested that the conference should consider the proposal inappropriate at the present time. The delegate of Brazil moved for adoption of such an amendment and commented on the rejection of a similar proposal by France and Spain at the Disarmament Conference of 1932. His motion was seconded by Correa of Ecuador. The delegate of Afghanistan supported the New Zealand-Australia proposal as conducive to a more peaceful world, and Hymans of France expressed agreement with his views. Speaking for the United States, Adolf Berle supported the Brazilian amendment. He ended the debate with an eloquent statement of regret that the world was not ready for what had been proposed and the need for other means of achieving peaceful aims. The Brazilian amendment was then adopted on a voice vote with an evident strong majority, and Chairman Martin declared the issue settled.

Before that plenary session of Committee I adjourned in the late afternoon of 8 November, Chairman Martin noted that all three subcommittees had met and organized, and each had completed a first reading of the proposals submitted to it. He proposed a motion authorizing him to appoint one or more drafting committees that could assist in harmonizing differences among the subcommittees and assist Committee I generally. He also proposed that amendments to the draft conventions under consideration should be submitted as soon as possible and prior to their day of consideration. His motion was accepted, and the meeting adjourned. The need for a drafting committee had already become apparent in the work of subcommittees 1 and 3, both of which had been assigned portions of the Canadian draft convention. Their discussions inevitably involved the conflicting views of the United States, Canada, and the United Kingdom. Subcommittee 1, of which Viscount Alain du Parc of Belgium was chairman and I was secretary, made little progress in its early meetings. Subcommittee 3, of which H. J. Symington of Canada was chairman and Melvin A. Brenner of the United States Civil Aeronautics Board was secretary, soon came to an impasse over the provisions in the Canadian draft convention for economic regulation by an international authority.

On 10 and 11 November, the two subcommittees met jointly, with Symington serving as chairman and Viscount du Parc as co-chairman. Both meetings attempted to deal with the provisions of the Canadian draft on which there was little disagreement. The resulting discussion, article by article, led to considerable clarification of views and many suggestions for redrafting, all of which were referred to the drafting committee that had been appointed.

That drafting committee consisted of G. G. FitzMaurice, United Kingdom, chairman; Lt. Col. W. F. Hodgson, Australia; E. P. Barbosa da Silva, Brazil; Escott Reid, Canada; and Livingston Satterthwaite, United States. With some changes in composition when reconstituted, this drafting committee, on which I served as secretary, was involved in much of the further work of the conference. It cleaned up the draft provisions previously discussed in subcommittees 1 and 3, separately or jointly, and that work may have been of assistance when the ABC talks, then about to begin, reached the point of putting something in draft form.

Meanwhile, subcommittee 2, Air Navigation Principles, with Chairman L. Welch Pogue presiding and Secretary Virginia C. Little assisting, had found its assignment to update much of the Paris and Havana Conventions agreeable and not very controversial. It worked hard at its third, fourth, and fifth meetings, on 8, 10, and 11 November, at which it completed substantially a first and second reading and revision of the assigned portions of the updated American draft of a convention. A drafting committee, consisting of John Cooper, United States, chairman; Luis Machado, Cuba; and Sir Frederick Tymms, India; was appointed, with Virginia C. Little as secretary and given the task of completing the text on the basis of the subcommittee's discussions.

A sixth meeting of the subcommittee was held on 15 November. At the time Chairman Pogue was busy elsewhere, and Viscount du Parc presided at the request of Mr. Martin. It was announced that Joseph Nisot (Belgium) had been added to the drafting committee.

Chairman Pogue returned to the seventh, eight, and ninth meetings on 21, 23, and 30 November, in each of which reports of the drafting committee were received, discussed, and referred back to it. At Chairman Pogue's request, Edward Warner introduced Albert Roper, secretary general of the prewar organization, at the meeting on 21 November, and he served thereafter as an adviser. At the final meeting on 30 November, a near final text was reviewed article by article, amended in minor respects, and given back to the drafting committee with authority to prepare it for presentation to a plenary session of the conference. It eventually became Part I, Air Navigation, of the Convention on International Civil Aviation.

The Conference During the ABC Talks

Early in the week beginning on Sunday, 12 November, it became apparent that work had come to a dead halt in the subcommittees of committees I, III, and IV. Representatives of the United States, United Kingdom, and Canada were holding private discussions in an effort to resolve their differences. These tripartite meetings were generally known at the conference as the ABC talks, for America, Britain, and Canada.

"In view of the obvious conflict of views—a conflict which was known before the conference—the question is not why the tripartite talks occurred, but why they occurred as late as they did. The probable explanation is that the United States was not ready to enter the tripartite talks until November 12," as Virginia Little commented in a dissertation for her Yale Ph.D. in 1948. Strategy had been planned by Adolf Berle and his colleagues on the assumption that the U.S.S.R. would attend and support the United States opposition to international economic regulation. The split within the United States delegation between executive and legislative members after arriving in Chicago was another and more immediate reason. No congressional representatives had participated in the preconference discussions with the British and Canadians, and none of them participated in the ABC talks at the conference.

A Review of the Work at the Chicago Conference

Senators Bailey and Brewster returned to Washington for the opening of Congress just after the beginning of the ABC talks, but were said to have made it clear to other members of the United States Delegation and to foreign delegates that under existing law the United States could not agree to an international body with economic regulatory power unless it were done by treaty subject to Senate ratification, which would involve a long and hard fight.

At a press conference on Tuesday, 14 November, Adolf Berle stated that the talks had been going on since 4:30 p.m., Sunday. He hoped for an agreement the following day but said he could make no public statement about the matters discussed At a press conference the following day, Adolf Berle introduced Mayor Fiorello La Guardia of New York, a member of the United States Delegation not often present. A somewhat humorous discussion ensued on Chicago versus New York as a possible airport of entry. Chicago had been omitted as a starting point for any of the international routes the CAB was considering. Hughes also reported in the *Tribune*, citing no source, that the results of the ABC talks had been turned over to a drafting committee, which would produce something for the further consideration of the principals. The following day, Hughes reported on some leakage from the drafting committee indicating difficulty in finding agreed language on pick-up traffic, quotas, and an escalator clause that would allow airlines flying at 65 percent of capacity to add frequencies of scheduled flights. Not much more of interest got into the press until the ABC talks broke up on the weekend in an apparent agreement to disagree.

During that week, most of the nontechnical members of the Secretariat and most members of the delegations were at loose ends, with much frustration developing. I myself had no official responsibilities for the time being and spent time reading newspapers and visiting parks, museums, and bookstores. I do recall one late evening party of mixed composition at which Escott Reid of the Canadian Delegation was present. In telling stories about the early days of the Canadian Foreign Office, which was not very old, he told about being sent to an Inter-American Conference. In the hotel bar after arrival, he heard various Latin American delegates kidding each other over the fulsome terms in which their qualifications would be described in the credentials they would read from the rostrum at the first meeting of the conference. Reid then suddenly realized that he had never been provided with an official credential. Whereupon, he retreated to his hotel room and wrote a suitable credential, which he duly read from the rostrum the following day.

Years later, I arrived in London in 1949 as chairman of the United States Delegation to the Second International Conference on North Atlantic Ocean Weather Stations, an ICAO conference. I learned that there would be a contested vote on some issue at the first plenary session. I was aware that the Department of State, in its usual stately fashion, had not yet provided me with the kind of credential to which I was entitled. But I remembered the Escott Reid story and also that I was already accredited to the Council in Montreal as an alternate representative of the United States. So, on my official stationery, I wrote a letter to the secretary of the conference, informing him that I had been designated to represent the United States. The secretary, my old friend, Edward Weld, chief of the Economic Bureau in Montreal, found this perfectly acceptable, and I was duly accredited. Ten days later I received a formal credential testifying to my integrity, prudence, and so forth signed by President Harry S. Truman and countersigned by Dean Acheson, secretary of state. With this in hand, I eventually signed the international agreement on behalf of the United States.

The Conference After the ABC Talks

By the end of the week of the ABC talks, it was clear that those talks could no longer be permitted to delay the rest of the conference by their private interminable arguments. On Sunday, their drafting committee put the final touches on part of a proposed permanent convention intended for distribution the following day. On some of the articles in the partial draft convention, there had been little disagreement but many reflected compromise. On some of the basic issues dividing the principals, the draft convention contained only titles for proposed articles in which the provisions were omitted. This was the locally famous document 358, "Section of An International Air Convention Relating Primarily to Air

Transport." When released on Monday, 20 November, it immediately created something of an uproar throughout the conference.

That same day, Adolf Berle was reported to have asked certain Latin American delegations to introduce a resolution at the coming plenary meeting that would leave all undecided questions to the proposed Interim Council. They refused and declared publicly that they desired 24 hours to study the new document.

On Wednesday, 22 November, Adolf Berle convened a joint plenary session of committees I, III, and IV, presiding with the consent of the other two committee chairmen. Whether this meeting was open to the press is not clear. Both Frank Hughes of the *Tribune* on 23 November and Russell Porter of the *Times* on 24 November had long stories on the plenary session and the joint subcommittee it created, but neither story was completely accurate or seems to reflect actual presence at the meeting.

Berle led off with a review of how much had been accomplished in the tripartite talks and elsewhere in the conference and proposed the creation of a joint subcommittee of committees I, III, and IV to work further on Document 358, to prepare a place for the work of subcommittee 2 of Committee I, and to coordinate with Committee IV on the completion of the Interim Agreement. Lord Swinton followed for the United Kingdom and began by paying tribute to the "United States Secretariat for their untiring work and help. If it is true that an army marches on its stomach, it is equally true that a conference marches on its secretariat. . . ." He thanked the United States for having convened the conference, expressed regret at the possibility of failure in some respects, but spoke at length on the magnitude of what had already been accomplished. He looked forward to further progress that could be accomplished under the Interim Agreement. He did not second the proposal to refer Document 358 to the proposed joint subcommittee, and seemed prepared to end the conference. Symington of Canada in his role as conciliator shared in Lord Swinton's felicitations and assessment of accomplishments but argued strongly that it was still possible to reach agreement on unsolved matters and complete a satisfactory convention.

Berle welcomed Symington's support and reported that the group representing the American Republics had met. He asked for a statement of their position. This was provided by Machado of Cuba, secretary of the Latin American informal organization. He noted that they had not been able to obtain a Spanish copy of Document 358 until that day, that it contained proposals needing further study and many on which delegations would wish to consult their governments. He reasserted the principle of juridical equality of all states and the need to protect the interests of small states in any international organization. He asked for further delay in taking up Document 358.

Berle responded that there would be ample time for study and consultation during the work of the proposed joint subcommittee. He then recognized the Delegate of the Netherlands, Mr. Steenberghe, chairman of Committee II. Steenberghe reported what had been agreed on by the parties in Document 358, regretted the omitted articles, and recalled the amount of technical work that had occurred in his committee that needed continuation under an international body. China was recognized next and supported the continuation of the work of the conference by establishing the proposed Interim Commission.

The delegate of Australia, Arthur Drakeford, then asked if this was the time for an expression of their views. Berle invited him to proceed, and he did so at considerable length. He concluded by supporting the hope of Canada that more could be accomplished before the conference adjourned. He was followed by Sullivan of New Zealand, who commented that he was in the unusual position of being in agreement with almost all that had been said, unlike the Irishman who, landing on foreign soil, asked, "Is there a government here? Because if there is, I'm agin it." Still, after speaking at some length, he joined in supporting the position of Canada.

Greece was recognized next and suggested that arrangements for the provisional organization should be completed before proceeding with Document 358. Berle again provided assurances on what could be done in the joint subcommittee. He then called on his old friend Mayor Fiorello La Guardia of the United States Delegation to close the discussion.

La Guardia then made a stem-winding speech that has sometimes been credited with turning the conference around when it was about to adjourn in failure. He referred to the noble objectives of the proposed convention's preamble but pointed out that the space was blank under Article II, Section 3, Freedoms of the air. With this omission, the convention was all sauce but no meat. In the strongest terms, he urged more effort to achieve unanimity on an agreement that would be fair to small countries as well as large and that could be completed before the conference adjourned.

Berle closed the meeting by proposing that committees I, III, and IV resolve themselves into a joint subcommittee under the chairmanship of John Martin, chairman of Committee I, to consider the document coming out of the tripartite talks, Document 358, and all problems relevant to it, in coordination with the concluding work on the Interim Agreement in Committee IV. The joint subcommittee should meet at the call of the chairman, but as soon as possible. This was agreed to, and the meeting was adjourned.

On the following day, Thursday, 23 November, Committee II held its final plenary session, Committee IV's joint subcommittee gave instructions to its drafting committee for completing its work, and Welch Pogue's subcommittee 2 of Committee I met in a near final session, all as previously noted.

Work in the Joint Subcommittee of Committees I, III, and IV

The first meeting of the new joint subcommittee was not convened by chairman John Martin until Friday, 24 November. I was called on to serve as secretary, with Virginia Little assisting. So far as I was aware, no duties in connection with the joint subcommittee were assigned to the secretaries and assistant secretaries of committees III and IV. A drafting committee was authorized and consisted mainly of names already familiar: F. C. Aronstein (Netherlands), chairman; Lt. Col. Hodgson (Australia); E. P. Barbara da Silva (Brazil); J. R. Baldwin (Canada); R. Aglion (France); G. G. FitzMaurice (United Kingdom); and S. W. Morgan (United States), with me as secretary. This drafting committee served until the end of the conference, and with the drafting committee of Welch Pogue's subcommittee 2, was jointly responsible for putting the convention together in its final form.

Paul T. David

The joint subcommittee began reading Document 358, article by article, for approval or amendment at its first meeting. It quickly provided for an Air Navigation Committee and an Air Transport Committee under what was still called the Board. The Board was enlarged from 14 to 21 members, and a third category of states was suggested, those making the largest contribution of facilities to air navigation. The Board was authorized to elect its own chairman, who would serve without vote. Having spent most of its time on the first four articles, the meeting agreed to meet at 10:00 a.m. the following day and adjourned at about 5:00 p.m. It had recessed for lunch from 12:50 p.m. to 2:45 p.m. Almost all chief delegates had been present, some with advisers, which meant over 50 people in the room at all times. It was clear that each article would receive meticulous attention, with amendments and alternative drafts offered with some frequency.

Virginia Little and I were busy taking notes throughout the day, and it became obvious that a series of long working sessions was ahead. After a quick meal, Virginia and I spent the evening writing the minutes of the meeting and marking up the document for changes agreed upon or suggested. By 11:00 p.m., the draft minutes were in the conference's reproduction shop, where five high-speed multigraph machines produced copies for all delegations by breakfast time the following morning. This pattern of working sessions with large attendance, followed by hours of work on minutes and documents by the secretariat, persisted at the second meeting on Saturday, which adjourned after 6:00 p.m., and again at some of the daily meetings of the committee the following week. A stenographic transcript was probably being taken of the meetings, but was not available in time to be helpful and was not published.

At the second meeting, the use of "Council" rather than "Board" was suggested, the three categories of members of a Council of 21 were clarified, and the chairman suggested that the Conference Steering Committee might begin work on a proposed list of council members, for consideration by the Executive Committee of all delegation chairmen, and then by a plenary session of the conference. Before leaving Article IV, the council was authorized to appoint "a chief executive officer who shall be called the Secretary-General. . . ." The meeting then spent the rest of the day on the further articles, reaching the end of Document 358. It was completely redrafted over the weekend under the drafting committee chairmanship of F. C. Aronstein (Netherlands) and distributed as Document 402.

The main business on Monday, 27 November, however, was the consideration of the conflicting British and American views on the economic regulation of international air transport. Each had a document, distributed the previous week, presenting and discussing proposed drafts of articles omitted in Document 358. Each involved detailed provisions regarding the regulation of capacity offered on international air routes involving multiple commercial stops. The United States had moved a considerable distance in the direction of the United Kingdom position, but with a remaining total disagreement on the extent of freedom to pick up and transport between intermediate points on such routes.

In its document, the United States asserted that any agreement compatible with successful commercial operations "must make possible operation of 'through routes' by nations which may not have reserves of terminal traffic sufficient to make such routes feasible without intermediate traffic—if, indeed, any nation has reserves of terminal traffic great enough to permit them to operate routes without intermediate traffic." Probably in regard to the proposed heavy economic regulatory powers of the international body, the United States expressly refrained from any commitment and put its document forward primarily as a basis for further discussion.

After Lord Swinton and Adolf Berle had presented and defended the alternative concepts and provisions at the meeting, Berle asked for a statement of national views by each of those present. Such statements consumed the remainder of the day and the beginning of the next day's meeting. In the end it was clear that there was broad support for the United States position and not much for that of the United Kingdom. In her doctoral dissertation, Virginia Little tabulated 20 states for the United States position and five for the United Kingdom, including France, Belgium, Australia, and Uruguay. India and South Africa reserved their position, and New Zealand was "unclear." Canada was listed as supporting the United States but really offered a compromise. Uruguay apologized for deserting its continental neighbors, and Norway, although listed as supporting the United States position, actually spoke for the Canadian compromise.

The meeting of the joint subcommittee on 27 November was in many ways the decisive point of the conference. This was true even though representatives of 26 of the 54 nations represented had refrained from making any statement of position, probably because of indecision on the part of their governments and some reluctance to offend either protagonist. But it was clear that the United Kingdom's desire for economic regulation of international air transport could not become a part of the convention. On the other hand, it was equally clear that the United Kingdom would refuse to sign any convention including unlimited rights for pickup traffic at intermediate points and was reluctant to include any statement on freedoms of the air in the permanent convention in the absence of the desired economic regulatory powers.

For differing reasons, many other countries were reluctant to put such rights into the convention. The result, as the conference went on, was the decision to prepare two separate agreements that were opened for signature in the Final Act: the International Air Transport Agreement ("the five freedoms agreement") and the International Air Services Transit Agreement ("the two freedoms agreement"). The second eventually achieved wide acceptance. The first was never a success and was eventually abandoned by most signatories, including the United States.

But the work on drafting the convention went on for several days before the need to pull out the provisions of the two separate agreements became apparent and was accepted. At the joint subcommittee meeting of 28 November, when the first redraft of Document 358 was taken up (Document 402), it was acted on, article by article, rather quickly and the meeting was able to adjourn at midday, to meet at 10:00 a.m. the following morning. Overnight, a second revised draft, Document 422, was produced and distributed. It was reviewed at a morning meeting on 29 November, but the most important occurrence was the giving of notice by the United States that it would seek action the next day on the articles omitted from the original Document 358.

A Review of the Work at the Chicago Conference

At another morning meeting on 30 November, action on the United States motion was deferred, but a United Kingdom motion to refer most of the important unfinished business to the Interim Council was seconded by the United States and approved. At an evening meeting at 9:30 p.m. that same day, the United States' motion to delete several of the contested articles was adopted. A first version of the International Air Transport Agreement as proposed by the United States (Document 446) was also approved, with almost no discussion. It later received two revisions without any change in its major intent. The meeting adjourned after agreeing to meet the next day to consider Document 442, the third revised draft of Document 358.

At the chairman's request, I reported for the drafting committee at the morning meeting of 1 December. Two alternative provisions for the composition of the Air Navigation Commission were offered in Article IV-A, Section 1. Edward Warner, reporting delegate of Committee II, moved for the second alternative, a commission of 12 highly qualified experts, which was approved. The title of the presiding officer of the council was changed from "chairman" to "president." A few other major provisions were included, revised, or referred back to the drafting committee. At this eighth meeting of the joint subcommittee, its work was considered substantially complete, the Secretariat and drafting committee were thanked, and the meeting adjourned. . . .

Final Plenary Sessions

A transcript of that Executive Committee meeting on 4 December has not been published and was not available at the time. It left the Secretariat unaware of decisions that could have gone into the drafting work overnight. Later the next day, President Berle referred to the Drafting Committee as having worked all night, followed by the Coordinating Committee as having been at work all day, presumably laying out the proposed Final Act and arranging the documents to go in it.

The Third Plenary session of the conference, intended to complete all paperwork for the Final Act and leaving nothing for further revision, did not convene until the evening of 5 December, with the expectation that the final plenary session would occur on 7 December. Dr. Warren Kelchner, the secretary general of the conference, had insisted that he required two days to have the Final Act typed as a set of documents ready for signature.

John Martin was called on first to report as chairman of Committee I. He presented the convention as ready for final approval as Appendix II of the Final Act, and then the final version of the International Air Transport Agreement, to become Appendix IV. Both were approved forthwith.

The report of Committee II was presented next, with a commentary by the reporting delegate, Dr. Warner, who also presented three proposed resolutions, one on the status of the Draft Technical Annexes, one on Technical Personnel, and one on the metric system, which were approved as Resolutions II, III, and IV in the Final Act. Warner commented that most of the states participating in the conference had representatives on a majority of the subcommittees, and a number were represented on all ten. The technical work accomplished would have worldwide consequences.

With Committee II's work approved, President Berle found it necessary to take the conference back to Article 45 of the convention as adopted, which had left open the seat of the permanent organization. Sitting next to him at the Rostrum, I had passed up a note calling attention to the oversight. Berle then stated that the subject had been much discussed at the previous Executive Committee meeting, and the two countries most concerned had since reached an agreement. He then called on Symington of Canada, who moved to amend Article 45 to provide that the seat of the permanent organization be left to determination at the final meeting of the Interim Assembly. Berle then read a text of the proposed amendment as it appears in the convention and called on Max Mymans of the French Delegation. Speaking in French, Hymans paid tribute to the contributions of Canada during the war and its willingness to provide a home for the Interim Council. He seconded the motion to amend Article 45, and it was immediately agreed.

Berle also suggested a redrafting of the signature clause at the end of the convention to remove any time limit on the period for signature. This was agreed and had probably been brought on by an inability to agree on a time limit in the Executive Committee.

Berle reported for Committee III, of which he had been chairman. He noted the continuing need for bilateral arrangements on air routes and the amount of work that had gone into developing a recommended standard form of agreement. This was approved and became Resolution VIII of the Final Act.

Chairman Guimaraes of Committee IV sought approval for the final text of the Interim Agreement on International Civil Aviation. It was accepted as Appendix I of the Final Act.

Various matters coming out of the joint work of committees I, III, and IV were then disposed of, including the legal matters that became Resolutions V, VI, and VII of the Final Act. Resolution X recommending transfer of unresolved issues to the Interim Council was approved.

The International Air Services Transit Agreement was then taken up. It was given a slight word change, at the insistence of the United Kingdom, to make it certain that the rights of transit and nontraffic stop that it offered would be available only to scheduled international air services. It was then approved as Appendix III of the Final Act.

Another action coming out of the Executive Committee was noted. It provided that in the final clause stating that the convention had been "Done at Chicago, on the seventh day of December, 1944, in the English Language," the following statement should be added: "A text drawn up in the English, French, and Spanish languages, each of which shall be of equal authenticity, shall be opened for signature at Washington, D.C." (The task of creating a Spanish text that the various Latin American countries could agree on required years of effort.)

The formalities of approving Resolutions I, IX, and XI then occurred; the first authorized preparation of the Final Act. The ninth, coming from the Executive Committee, requested PICAO to consider alternative languages that might be used in flight documents in relevant regions of the world. The eleventh authorized the United States to publish the Final Act and other documents serving the public interest, obviously including the two volume *Proceedings* so much referred to herein. They did not appear until 1948 and 1949, after the convention had come into effect on 4 April 1947.

President Berle then announced a meeting of the Executive Committee the following day to elect members of the Interim Council.

Sir Arthur Street of the United Kingdom was then called on to present the closing resolution thanking everyone for everything. Hymans of France seconded, and that near final plenary session closed in general agreement at 9:22 p.m.

At the Executive Session the next day, no members of the Secretariat were present except Theodore Wright, the technical secretary, and Dr. Warren Kelchner, the secretary general, but the minutes were published in the conference's daily *Journal* and in the *Proceedings*. The three categories of the Interim Council members were to be voted on separately and in sequence by secret ballot. Tellers were appointed and Dr. Kelchner was responsible for the count under their supervision. The following states were elected as members of Category A, Air Transport: United Kingdom, United States, Netherlands, Brazil, France, Mexico, and Belgium. On the second balloting for Category B, Navigational Facilities, Canada, Cuba, Norway, Iraq, and Peru were elected. On the third balloting for Category C, Geographical Representation, China, Australia, Egypt, Czechoslovakia, Turkey, El Salvador, Chile, and Columbia were elected. The election was thereupon declared closed, final, and incontestable.

President Berle then announced that the Final Act would be open for signature early the following day, 7 December, followed immediately by the Final Plenary Session of the conference. He also announced that signers of the "five freedoms agreement" should also feel free to sign the "two freedoms agreement" if they were willing to do so. The meeting then adjourned.

The omission of India from those elected to the Interim Council evidently brought on an overnight crisis resulting in some doubt over whether either India or the United Kingdom would sign the Final Act. That problem was resolved at the opening of the final plenary session the next day. Ambassador Morgenstierne of Norway, acting on his own initiative and without consulting his government, but after consultation with representatives of the other

Scandinavian states, requested unanimous consent to permit India to replace Norway on the Interim Council. Berle noted the act as one of great magnanimity and recognized the delegate of Cuba, Felipe Pazos. Pazos said that he had received notice of the intentions of Norway only ten minutes before but would nevertheless offer the resignation of Cuba and request withdrawal of the Norwegian resignation. After further graceful remarks by Berle, Morgenstierne expressed total surprise and great appreciation, noting that with the change, which he accepted, Latin America and Europe would each have six seats on the Council instead of a proportion of seven to five. India was then voted unanimously into the now vacant seat. Cuba was given a special vote of thanks, and the secretary general was directed to send an appropriate message to the government of Cuba.

The conference was then ready for final oratory. It heard first from Dr. Chang of China, a vice president of the conference, who expressed great appreciation for what had been accomplished. (The other vice president, Hymans of France, refrained from speaking on this occasion.) Lord Swinton then spoke to the three sections of Resolution XII that had been offered by Sir Arthur Street in his absence. He expanded on each of the three: the first on appreciation to that great leader, President Roosevelt, for convening this conference; the second on the untiring work and helpfulness of the president of the conference, Adolf Berle, and other members of the United States Delegation; and third, his appreciation and gratitude to all of the members of the Secretariat who had worked with so much efficiency and expedition. Adolf Berle then made the closing address in which he predicted how much the world would change as the result of what had been accomplished at this conference. He paid tribute to the delegations of the United Kingdom and Canada, noting that the latter had produced the language and the phrase on "the freedoms of the air." The chairmen of the major committees other than his own, John Martin, M. P. L. Steenberghe, and Hahneman Guimaraes, were singled out for special thanks. He ended by quoting some Biblical words of King David and adjourned the conference at noon, Thursday, 7 December 1944.

CHAPTER THIRTEEN

A Personal Appreciation: Paul T. David

Kenneth W. Thompson

Paul David taught us all that life can begin at 80, much as his wife Opal had taught us earlier that being a two-term Albemarle county supervisor can begin at 69. I could go on about Opal, who is one of the most remarkably gracious and effective community leaders I've ever known, but this is an appreciation of Paul. Iron resolve and unflagging idealism ran throughout his career. He had been raised in a parsonage and became politically and socially conscious at Antioch. Long after it ceased being fashionable, he remained an unabashed liberal. I'm not sure he ever quite realized that the ideological climate had changed. If he did, he saw no reason for reshaping his personality or his beliefs. Paul had difficulty recognizing that people differed with him—politically, administratively, or in his vision of education. If he recognized it, he saw no reason for tailoring his views to fit their cloth. He could remain silent for long periods in discussion groups, but if you pressed the right button, he was off. Five or ten minutes later, or so it seemed to those of us who were closest to him—not least Opal—he had finished and reverted to the role of patient listener.

I may be wrong, but Paul was one of a handful of friends who wasn't afraid to discuss any of the chapters in his scholarly or governmental life. Most of us draw no pleasure from rehearsing experiences that didn't turn out as we hoped. Paul was much briefer in reviewing those chapters, but he had few remembrances that were forbidden territory. For most undertakings, he had instant recall and seemingly a photographic memory. He recalled names, places, events, and institutions. Since they were important historically, however remote, he assumed they were important to everyone else. He had been a participant in important years of the New Deal and the development of political science and political economy. It came naturally for him to discuss what he had seen and done. Often despite age or ideological mind-sets, the powerful and the mighty of the new era learned from Paul.

Paul had an ability to work with others that not everyone recognized. He participated and sometimes led major group activities. Laurin Henry has reported on Paul's part in the recommendations of the American Political Science Association's Committee on Political Parties (see chapters 9 and 10). In 1951 he directed a study of the Administration of Foreign Affairs and Overseas Operations for the Brookings Institution. In 1952 he organized a joint study for the same center in collaboration with the American Political Science Association. It led to an unprecedented five-volume publication, *Presidential Nominating Politics*, in 1952. He and two co-authors drew on the data of 70 collaborators from their respective states. Another cooperative study followed: *The Politics of National Party Conventions*.

All of these achievements were grist for the mill of at least three Miller Center commissions after Paul modestly suggested he had some information that might be useful. He would photocopy the material, turn up the books, and bring the citations to my office. This was the other side of his personality. If on one side he sometimes seemed oblivious to the reactions of others with whom he was associated, he also had a record of leadership in the organization of major scholarly enterprises that few can match. Somehow that never quite got through to his detractors, and I'm not sure why. Perhaps it was because he featured the organization and its actions, not himself, when he talked about work and achievements.

In his final months and days he had his sad moments. When he accompanied me to Washington for meetings of the Miller

Kenneth W. Thompson

Center Commission on the Selection of Vice Presidents, he was visibly tired from the trip. When the commission convened, most of the younger commission members knew nothing of his work. Paul sat silently and even dozed off from time to time. Then suddenly a commission member who was Paul's contemporary spoke of his many studies. Long-time friend and associate Ambassador Max Kampelman intervened and said, "Paul David is the world's authority on that subject. Let's hear from him." Paul answered with clarity and precision, drawing on a great fund of knowledge. The commission moved on, and Paul was forgotten. He was in no way resentful; it had happened before. For a few brief moments he was indeed the world's authority, but on the drive back to Charlottesville he napped once more. It happens to us all. The world moves on.

After such experiences, most senior scholars would have continued to nap and sleep. Not Paul. He took such experiences in stride, labored on, and spun off new ideas and proposals as if he were 40. He was considerate of others. One day he brought in a dietary preparation that he said he had used himself. Perhaps I'd want to try it. Paul had about him a touch of intellectual immortality. He had more to do, miles to go before he slept. He never gave up. He and Opal are among the Center's most generous supporters, but their greatest gift has not been money. They are wellsprings of ideas. They occupy a very important place in the Center's history. Our successors must take up their torch and not grow weary. Paul left an example for them to follow.